CW00847259

ENGLISH CURSIVE BOOK HANDS

1250–1500

M. B. PARKES

SCOLAR PRESS

Scolar Press
90/91 Great Russell Street
London WC1B 3PY

Copyright © Oxford University Press, 1969, and M. B. Parkes, 1979

First published 1969 by Oxford University Press
Reprinted (with minor revisions) by Scolar Press, 1979

British Library Cataloguing in Publication Data

Parkes, Malcolm Beckwith
English cursive book hands, 1250–1500. – 1st ed. reprinted with minor revisions.
1. Paleography, English
I. Title
745.6′1 Z115.E5
ISBN 0-85967-535-1

Printed in Great Britain by
The Scolar Press
Ilkley, West Yorkshire

FOR PAM

PREFACE

THIS is intended to be a teaching book. The emphasis is entirely upon the major varieties of English cursive handwriting in this period, and the principal developments which took place in them. Unfortunately limitations of space have prevented any discussion of abbreviations used by the scribes, or of changes in the format of manuscripts, but the reader will find some observations on these topics in the notes to the plates. References in the footnotes and the notes to the plates are not intended to be exhaustive, but to provide a starting-point for further inquiries. For the benefit of the student I have included notes on the terminology I have used and on the transcriptions.

Where possible I have preferred to choose a plate from a dated or a datable manuscript, even though this has meant that occasionally I have had to include a plate from a manuscript which has already been reproduced elsewhere. However, since most of the manuscripts which I have used to illustrate Secretary book hands are undated, I have included a sequence of extracts from documents to illustrate the criteria for dating. I am conscious that in some cases a particular plate has been chosen to illustrate so many features that it fails to illustrate any one of them very well. All plates are reproduced to the actual size of the manuscript unless otherwise stated. Whenever possible I have referred to other reproductions which occur in printed books or collections of facsimiles. I have relied entirely upon such collections to illustrate the development of the Anglicana script in documents, and developments in French document hands.

I wish to thank all those colleagues who have patiently answered my questions. In particular I must single out Professor N. Davis, Dr. A. I. Doyle, Dr. R. W. Hunt, and Professor F. Wormald, who have not only furnished information but have advised, criticized, and corrected my errors at various stages. I owe a special debt to Mr. N. R. Ker: he not only supervised my early work on English handwriting but he has given advice at all stages since, and has helped me to clarify my ideas in the course of many vigorous discussions. For their patience, encouragement, and generosity with their time I am sincerely grateful. I remain solely responsible for the views expressed in this book.

I must also thank my pupils who have not only given most helpful advice about the presentation of the material from the reader's point of view but have also shared in the burden of checking my transcriptions. Although it is invidious to single out names, I must acknowledge a particular debt to Miss P. R. Robinson, because her pertinent criticisms and suggestions at an early stage helped me to formulate my ideas on the layout of the book.

M. B. P.

Keble College, Oxford
April 1969

PREFACE TO THE REPRINT

I HAVE taken advantage of the opportunity afforded by this reprint to make a number of corrections, and, where practicable, to bring certain references up to date: I have also added indexes. Nothing has so far come to light which seems to call for a fundamental revision of the book, and I have felt reluctant to tinker with minor points for fear of disturbing the balance. However, I have added references both in footnotes and in the Select Bibliography to some of the more pertinent recent studies. In 1973 the book, manuscript, and map Departments of the British Museum became divisions of the British Library, but it has proved impracticable to alter the location from 'British Museum' to 'British Library' in references to shelfmarks in the national collections.

M. B. P.

Keble College, Oxford
January 1979

CONTENTS

REFERENCES AND ABBREVIATIONS

References to the plates frequently include column (a or b), line number, and word. Thus Plate 6 (ii), a, 4 'thinges' indicates the word 'thinges' in line 4 of the first column in Plate 6 (ii).

The principal abbreviations used in the introduction and the notes to the plates are:

Allen (1927)	H. E. Allen, *Writings Ascribed to Richard Rolle, Hermit of Hampole* (London and New York, 1927).
Archiv	*Archiv für das Studium der neueren Sprachen und Literaturen* (1846–).
Bibl. Nat.	Paris, Bibliothèque Nationale.
Bodl.	Oxford, Bodleian Library.
Brit. Mus.	London, British Museum.
c.	*circa.*
Cat. Royal MSS.	G. F. Warner and J. P. Gilson, *Catalogue of Western Manuscripts in the Old Royal and King's Collections in the British Museum* (London, 1921).
Coxe	H. O. Coxe, *Catalogus Codicum MSS qui in Collegiis Aulisque Oxoniensibus hodie adservantur* (Oxford, 1852).
CPL.	E. Dekkers, 'Clavis Patrum Latinorum', *Sacris Erudiri*, iii (2nd edition, Bruges, 1961).
CSEL.	*Corpus Scriptorum Ecclesiasticorum Latinorum* (Vienna, 1866–).
CT.	Geoffrey Chaucer, 'The Canterbury Tales', ed. F. N. Robinson, *The Works of Geoffrey Chaucer* (2nd edition, London, 1957).
ECH.	C. Johnson and H. Jenkinson, *English Court Hand, A.D. 1066–1500* (Oxford, 1915), i, Text, ii, Plates.
ed.	edited by.
E.E.T.S. (E.S.)	Early English Text Society, Extra Series (London, 1867–1920).
E.E.T.S. (O.S.)	Early English Text Society, Original Series (London, 1864–).
Emden, *BRUC.*	A. B. Emden, *A Biographical Register of the University of Cambridge to 1500* (Cambridge, 1963).
Emden, *BRUO.*	A. B. Emden, *A Biographical Register of the University of Oxford to A.D. 1500* (Oxford, 1957–9).
fol.	folio.
Hammond (1908)	E. P. Hammond, *Chaucer, A Bibliographical Manual* (New York, 1908).
Index	C. Brown and R. H. Robbins, *The Index of Middle English Verse* (New York, 1943). *Supplement*, ed. R. H. Robbins and J. L. Cutler (Lexington, 1965).
James	M. R. James, *The Western Manuscripts in the Library of Trinity College, Cambridge, A Descriptive Catalogue* (Cambridge, 1900–4).
LCH.	H. Jenkinson, *The Later Court Hands in England* (Cambridge, 1927).
Mss. datés	C. Samaran and R. Marichal, *Catalogue des manuscrits en écriture latine, portant des indications de date de lieu ou de copiste* (Paris, 1959–).
N. Pal. Soc. i	New Palaeographical Society, *Facsimiles of Ancient MSS &c.*, ed. E. M. Thompson, G. F. Warner, F. G. Kenyon, and J. P. Gilson, 1st series (London, 1903–12).

N. Pal. Soc. ii	New Palaeographical Society, *Facsimiles of Ancient MSS &c.*, ed. E. M. Thompson, G. F. Warner, F. G. Kenyon, and J. P. Gilson, 2nd series (London, 1913–30).
OED.	*Oxford English Dictionary.*
O.H.S.	Oxford Historical Society.
Pal. Soc. i	Palaeographical Society, *Facsimiles of MSS. and Inscriptions*, ed. E. A. Bond, E. M. Thompson, and G. F. Warner, 1st series (London, 1873–83).
Pal. Soc. ii	Palaeographical Society, *Facsimiles of MSS. and Inscriptions*, ed. E. A. Bond, E. M. Thompson, and G. F. Warner, 2nd series (London, 1884–94).
PL.	*Patrologiae Cursus Completus*, series latina, accurante J. P. Migne.
Powicke, *MBMC.*	F. M. Powicke, *The Medieval Books of Merton College* (Oxford, 1931).
P.R.O.	London, Public Record Office.
RS.	Rolls Series; i.e. Rerum Britannicarum Medii Aevi Scriptores (London, 1858–96).
Sarton	G. Sarton, *Introduction to the History of Science, II. From Rabbi ben Ezra to Roger Bacon* (Washington, i (1927), ii (1931)).
SC.	*A Summary Catalogue of Western MSS. in the Bodleian Library at Oxford* (Oxford, 1895–1953).
sig.	signature.
STC.	A. W. Pollard and G. R. Redgrave, *A Short Title Catalogue of Books printed in England, Scotland and Ireland 1475–1640* (London, 1950).
Stegmüller, *Bibl.*	F. Stegmüller, *Repertorium Biblicum Medii Aevi* (Madrid, 1950–61).
Thorndike and Kibre	L. Thorndike and P. Kibre, *A Catalogue of Incipits of Medieval Scientific Writings in Latin* (rev. edition, 1963).
Ward, *Cat. Romances*	H. L. D. Ward and J. A. Herbert, *Catalogue of Romances in the Department of Manuscripts in the British Museum* (London, 1883–1910).
Wells	J. E. Wells, *A Manual of the Writings in Middle English, 1050–1400* (New Haven, 1926, and supplements).
Wright, *EVH.*	C. E. Wright, *English Vernacular Hands from the Twelfth to the Fifteenth Centuries* (Oxford, 1960).
Young and Aitken	J. Young and P. H. Aitken, *A Catalogue of the MSS. in the Library of the Hunterian Museum in the University of Glasgow* (Glasgow, 1908).

INTRODUCTION

FROM the mid twelfth century onwards, the nature of the developments which took place in English book hands was largely determined by two factors: the increasing demand for books, and the increase in the size of the works to be copied. The secularization of learning and the rise of the universities created a voracious demand for texts and commentaries. At the same time improving standards of literacy led to a demand from a wide range of patrons for books of a more general nature. The size of the commentaries upon the Bible, the 'Sentences', and the civil and canon law increased as each new generation enlarged upon the work of its predecessors; and in poetry, works like the 'Cursor Mundi' (some 30,000 lines) and the 'Roman de la Rose' (some 20,000 lines in its final form) imposed heavy demands upon the time and energy of the scribes who copied them. The reaction of a scribe to such demands is occasionally revealed in comments like the one found in the colophon of a fourteenth-century manuscript:

> Explicit secunda pars summe fratris thome de aquino ordinis fratrum predicatorum, longissima, prolixissima, et tediosissima scribenti; Deo gratias, Deo gratias, et iterum Deo gratias.[1]

In such circumstances speed and ease of writing came to be as important to the scribe who copied books as they had become to the scribe who prepared or drafted documents.[2] Scribes began to use different kinds of handwriting for different classes of books, and as a result a new 'hierarchy' of scripts arose, each with its own sequence of development. For finer-quality manuscripts, such as liturgical books in which the appearance of the book was a most important consideration, the scribes developed an elaborate, highly calligraphic 'display' script known as 'Textura'.[3] It gradually became more artificial, less affected by practical considerations, and in consequence less used, as time passed. But for more utilitarian volumes, the increasing demands upon the time and energy of the scribes and the need to conserve space led to the development of smaller, simpler hands both to keep books within a manageable format and to accelerate the process of production. At first they took as their model the handwriting used about 1200 for writing commentaries in the margins of texts.[4] From this they developed what are sometimes referred to nowadays as the smaller 'gothic' book hands,[5] which became highly compressed, closely spaced, and full of abbreviations.[6] The size and compression of the hands gave little scope for style, and the traditions of the earlier hands were

[1] Oxford, New College, MS. 121, fol. 376v.

[2] See *ECH.*, pp. xiv–xv.

[3] For accounts of the development of Textura see S. Morison, '*Black Letter*' *Text* (Cambridge, 1942); and R. W. Hunt's article 'Palaeography' in *Chambers' Encyclopaedia* (London, 1952), x. For a fifteenth-century example of the script see below Plate 22 (ii).

[4] For examples of the 'glossing hands' at this date see R. A. B. Mynors, *Durham Cathedral MSS. to the End of the Twelfth Century* (Oxford, 1939), pls. 43, 47; and Pal. Soc. i, pl. 37.

[5] For examples see *Cat. Royal MSS.*, pls. 37, 56 (c), 89 (a); *Facsimile of MS. Bodley 34*, E.E.T.S. (o.s.), 247; W. W. Greg, *Facsimiles of Twelve Early English MSS. in the Library of Trinity College, Cambridge* (Oxford, 1913), pls. v and vi; J. Destrez, *La Pecia dans les mss. universitaires du xiii*e *et du xiv*e *siècle* (Paris, 1935), pls. 27–31; and Wright, *EVH.*, pls. 10, 11.

[6] See below Plate 16 (ii).

soon abandoned. Later, towards the end of the thirteenth century, the cursive script which had recently been evolved for the preparation of documents was introduced into books.

A hierarchy also arose in the cursive script itself, as scribes began to devise more than one way of writing depending on the degree of formality they required. Scribes who drafted documents began to distinguish between the handwriting used for a document actually issued, the 'engrossing hand', and that used for the mere enrolment of a document for reference purposes.[1] The two ways of writing were taken up and adapted by scribes who wrote books, and the practice culminated in a major development in the hierarchy of scripts: the evolution of a hierarchy of varieties of a single script. Eventually the varieties of cursive usurped the functions of other scripts in the copying of nearly all kinds of books and documents. Some of these varieties lost their cursive nature, but all of them betray their cursive origin in the shapes of the letter forms and in the character of their calligraphy. The purpose of this book is to illustrate the developments which took place in the cursive handwriting used in England for writing books.

THE 'ANGLICANA' SCRIPT IN THE THIRTEENTH AND FOURTEENTH CENTURIES

The traditional English cursive script of the later Middle Ages was developed primarily from the current handwriting which arose in the course of preparing documents.[2] In order to write more rapidly, the scribe modified the duct[3] of his handwriting, wherever possible replacing straight strokes with curved ones which are more easily controlled when writing quickly. The scribe raised his pen from the surface as seldom as possible. Thus, as he manipulated the pen to trace the strokes of which the letters are composed, most of its movements were recorded upon the writing surface. The finishing movement of one stroke and the approach movement to the next tended to coalesce into a single movement which was recorded as a connecting stroke. This occurred not only between letters but also between the strokes which combined to make up a single letter, as, for example, in **f**, long-**s**, and in the ascender of **d**. These connecting strokes gradually came to be accepted as auxiliary features of the letter forms, thus becoming part of the morphology of the script. As a result of this process a set of distinctive letter forms emerged. At the same time the rapid duct became the basis of the style of the handwriting. The whole process took a long time, but when this stage had been reached, a cursive script had been evolved.[4]

A cursive script with recognizable characteristics of its own and which is recognizably akin to the later hands had emerged by the middle of the thirteenth century.[5] Its distinctive letter forms are: two-compartment **a**, with a large upper lobe extending

[1] See *ECH.*, pp. xiv–xv; L. C. Hector, *The Handwriting of English Documents* (London, 1966), p. 56.

[2] This development is illustrated in the frontispiece to vol. ii of *ECH.*, and ibid., pls. ii (c) and (d).

[3] The rise of the rapid duct may be followed in *ECH.*, pls. i (b) and (c). For an explanation of the terminology used in describing handwriting in this book see Note on Palaeographical Terms, p. xxvi.

[4] On the use of the term 'cursive' as applied to a category of script of this period see G. I. Lieftinck, 'Pour une nomenclature de l'écriture livresque de la période dite "gothique"', *Nomenclature des écritures livresques du ixe au xvie siècle* (Paris, 1954), p. 19.

[5] For example, *ECH.*, pl. xiii (b).

From about the third quarter of the fourteenth century onwards the history of English cursive handwriting was dominated by a new factor. A new cursive script was introduced into this country, a script which possessed letter forms and stylistic features which had no counterparts in the traditional English cursive handwriting.

Most of the elements, or basic strokes, which together make up the letter forms of this new script are common to all varieties of Anglicana. The most important distinctions between the new script and the established one lie in the duct of the script and in the treatment of strokes and letter forms (Plates 9 and 10). First, the duct of the new script was based upon the regular antithesis of broad strokes and hairlines placed in different diagonals according to the angle of the slanted pen, thus giving to many of the hands a characteristic 'splayed' appearance.[1] Secondly, angular broken strokes appeared in places where in most other scripts one would expect to find curved ones. This is most noticeable in the treatment of the lobes of the letters **a**, **d**, and **g**; in the formation of the letters **o** and '2'-shaped **r**; and in the treatment of the stems of the letters **c** and **e**. Occasionally this feature is blurred in current writing. Thirdly, 'horns' were frequently formed on the tops of the letters, especially **e**, **g**, **t**, and short final **s**, and at points of breaking. Fourthly, the tapering, sloping descenders of **f**, long-**s**, and **p** were exaggerated. Finally, the graphs of **a**, **g**, **r**, and short-**s** have no counterparts in any other contemporary English script.

The cursive short **r** form, more than any other feature, points to a continental origin for the new script. The ultimate place of origin is obscure, but was most probably Italy. A cursive script with a single compartment **a**, single compartment **g**, short **r**, and short-**s** may be seen in hands of the Italian chanceries of the thirteenth and fourteenth centuries, and of the Papal Chancery at Avignon in the fourteenth.[2] In the fourteenth century it appears in Italy as a book hand.[3] By the end of the fourteenth century the new script had spread all over northern Europe, and was widely used in both books and documents. The Italian examples, however, lack that distinctive treatment of the letter forms and other features of style which are characteristic of the new script, not only in England but in most of northern Europe. The script underwent some kind of modification before being imported into this country, and there can be little doubt that this took place in France.

The French scribes took the script and virtually transformed it. A version of the script, which was already more elaborate than the Italian hands, was well established by 1340 as the principal business hand of the north of France, particularly in and around Paris.[4] This version of the script was developed as a book hand during the course of the fourteenth century by incorporating features from that species of Textura which seems to me to be peculiar to French vernacular manuscripts of the period: in particular, features which later became characteristic of the new script in both France and England, such as the treatment of the minim strokes, a current form of the letter

[1] Cf. *LCH.*, pp. 51–8.

[2] See V. Federici, *La scrittura delle cancellerie italiane dal secolo xii al xvii* (Rome, 1934), tavv. xlvi, xlviii, lv–lviii. See also P. Chaplais, 'Master John de Branketre and the Office of Notary in Chancery 1355–1375', *Journal of the Society of Archivists*, iv (1971), 179, and pl. I.

[3] See *Mss. datés*, vol. i, pl. xliii; vol. ii, pls. xlv, liii; *Cat. Royal MSS.*, pl. 48.

[4] See *Receuil de facsimilés à l'usage de l'École des Chartes* (Paris, 1880–1901), nos. 81, 82, 100, 106.

r, and the form of two-compartment final short-**s**.[1] The earliest dated manuscript written in the new script which I have been able to discover so far (Bibl. Nat., MS. français 24305, dated 1356) does not contain these features, but in the hands of manuscripts produced in 1400[2] they have been so completely absorbed that they have become fundamental to the structure of the script. Thus, during the process of adapting the script for use as a book hand, the fluid mass of details became assimilated and co-ordinated into a new style of calligraphy the principal aim of which was to give harmony to the whole without losing the individuality of single letters.

One of the outstanding features of the history of English handwriting in the fifteenth century is the gradual infiltration of this new script, which in its English form we now call 'Secretary',[3] into all classes of books and documents, until by the sixteenth century it had become the principal script in use in this country. The emergence of the script can be traced in registers and documents. In the series of Archiepiscopal registers at Lambeth it first occurs in some entries in Archbishop Sudbury's Register (1375–81), and from 1396 onwards it remains the normal hand of the clerks until it was modified beyond recognition in the late seventeenth century. In the Archbishops' registers at York it appears in a notarial attestation dated 1379.[4] In the registers of the Bishops of London the script was firmly established by the time Bishop Walden's Register began in 1404. At Canterbury it already predominates in the earliest Register of Wills of the Consistory Court,[5] which begins in 1396, but among the records of the Prior and Convent, its first appearance is an entry in Registrum S, dated 1401. In the collection of Chancery Warrants[6] issued under the Privy Seal or Signet the new script is first used extensively in 1376, but it is hardly ever used in the other offices of the central government. Its early progress as a book hand is difficult to trace owing to a general absence of dated evidence. The script appears in a manuscript of Rolle's 'Emendatio Vitae', dated 1384,[7] and from a comparison between the hands of undated manuscripts and dated hands in documents, it is clear that it was well established as a book hand by 1400.

Until the mid fifteenth century the features of the handwriting underwent a series of rapid changes which reflect the uncertainty of scribes who were forced to master the forms and idiom of a new script. The early hands are stiff, upright, and ill proportioned (Plate 9 (i)). The more familiar Anglicana graphs of **a**, **g**, **r**, and short-**s** appear frequently in place of the new and consequently less well-known Secretary graphs (Plates 9 (i), 11 (ii)). Scribes tended to emphasize the various stylistic features in turn. Towards the end of the fourteenth century, in the more meticulous hands, elaborate broken strokes were introduced into the stems as well as the lobes of the letters (Plate 9 (ii)). In the first half of the fifteenth century scribes emphasized the horns which were formed at the tops of letters and at points of breaking, thus giving to the handwriting a characteristic 'prickly' appearance (Plates 10 (i), 11 (ii)). In the mid fifteenth century the letter forms were simplified, but the degree of splay was exaggerated (Plates 10 (ii), 12 (i)).

By this time the scribes had acquired greater familiarity with the new script. They were less affected by the precedents imposed by the graphs of Anglicana. Even the

[1] See *Mss. datés*, vol. i, pls. li (1364–73), lii (1368), lvii (1379); Pal. Soc. ii, pl. 168 (1371).

[2] For example, Bibl. Nat. MS. français 205 (dated 1400).

[3] On the Continent it is usually referred to as 'cursiva' (see G. I. Lieftinck, loc. cit.).

[4] See J. S. Purvis, *Notarial Signs from the York Archiepiscopal Records* (York, 1947), pl. 33.

[5] Maidstone, Kent County Archives Office, PRC/32/1.

[6] See *LCH*., pl. xxiii; Chaplais, *English Royal Documents*, p. 52.

[7] Brit. Mus. Add. MS. 34763, fols. 19–44.

large hooked ascenders to which they had been accustomed, and which are to be found frequently even in well-written Secretary hands of the first half of the century (Plates 11 (i), 11 (ii)), were replaced by the short ascenders with small rounded loops which are characteristic of the new script (Plates 10 (ii), 12 (i)). The scribes had also acquired greater fluency in its execution. During the second half of the century the hands are much more current: hairlines used in the construction of the letter forms were frequently omitted, but nevertheless details of style, such as the horns on the tops of the letters, were again emphasized (Plates 10 (iii), 12 (ii)). This combination of fluency and style afforded by the duct of the script, together with the fact that such Secretary forms as the ascenders, and the letters **a**, **g**, and **w** were easier to manage than the corresponding Anglicana forms when writing quickly, must have contributed to the scribes' increasing preference for the script.[1]

Towards the end of the century new features appear in the hands, which can be traced to further developments which had taken place in France during the fifteenth century.[2] The most prominent of these features are the new forms of **c** and short-**s**, and the exaggeration of the horns at the tops of the letters (Plate 13 (ii)). The development of the horns affected the structure of certain letter forms, notably **e** and **t**, and culminated in the appearance of the 'attacking strokes' which are so characteristic of the sixteenth-century hands.[3]

'BASTARD SECRETARY'

As with Anglicana in the fourteenth century, so with Secretary in the fifteenth, scribes developed a 'Bastard' variety of the script for use in formal contexts. The earliest attempts to produce a formal hand were influenced by Bastard Anglicana (Plate 14 (i)), but as the century advanced this ingredient was dropped from the mixture. The scribes then constructed large, well-spaced, calligraphic hands containing the typical 'Bastard' combination: cursive forms and features (this time derived from Secretary) with the proportions and stylistic features of Textura superimposed upon them (Plate 14 (ii)). The hands often appear stiff, since the details of the two scripts are not fully assimilated.

During the second half of the century the attempts of English scribes to evolve a Bastard variety of the script were overtaken by parallel developments which had been taking place on the Continent. These developments were based on that species of Textura which seems to be peculiar to French vernacular manuscripts, and culminated in the '*Lettre Bastarde*' found in manuscripts produced at the court of Burgundy.[4]

[1] The new script does not predominate among the entries of the 'Common Paper' (The Ordinance, court minute, and admissions book) of the Scriveners' Company of London (now London, Guildhall MS. 5370) until after 1440 (see *LCH*.). Of thirty-nine fifteenth-century manuscripts in the Bodleian Library containing works by Chaucer, Lydgate, and Gower, sixteen were written in the Secretary Script. From palaeographical criteria described in this book, eleven of these sixteen manuscripts may be assigned to the second half of the fifteenth century: MSS. Bodley 414, Laud Misc. 600, Rawl. Poet. 163, Rawl. Poet. 223, Trinity Coll. 49, and Arch. Seld. B. 24 (Plate 13 (ii)) (Chaucer); Ashmole 35 (Gower); Bodley 263, Douce 148, Rawl. C. 48, and Rawl. Poet. 144 (fols. 332–end) (Lydgate).

[2] See *Receuil de facsimilés à l'usage de l'École des Chartes*, nos. 77, 80, 90, 92, 99, 111; E. Poulle, *Paléographie des écritures cursives en France du xve au xviie siècle* (Geneva, 1966), pls. i–iv.

[3] For example, the initial strokes of the letters **a** and **t** (see C. B. Judge, *Specimens of Sixteenth Century English Handwriting* (Harvard, 1935), pl. vi), and the second stroke of **e** (ibid., pl. xv).

[4] For example, *Cat. Royal MSS.*, pls. 86, 87, 106.

During the second half of the fifteenth century the influence of these developments may be seen in English manuscripts (Plate 15 (i)), and by the first quarter of the sixteenth century English scribes had adopted the new French models (Plate 15 (ii)). The most obvious structural feature of these late hands is the replacement of the broken strokes in the lobes of the letters **a**, **d**, **g**, and the stems of **c** and **e** by a calligraphically formed curve. In this form the Bastard variety was used in sixteenth-century manuscripts (Plate 20 (ii)) and appears as one of the models in Baildon and Beauchesne's *A Booke Containing Divers Sortes of Hands*, published in 1571.[1]

ANGLICANA IN THE LATE FOURTEENTH AND THE FIFTEENTH CENTURIES

The primary importance of Secretary between 1375 and 1450 is that it was the means by which developments in the calligraphy of cursive handwriting which had taken place in France during the fourteenth century were transmitted to the established cursive script of this country. The impact of the new style of calligraphy had a profound effect upon the development of Anglicana, and led to the modification of the letter forms of the script.

The first indication of the new style in manuscripts written in ordinary Anglicana is the exaggeration of the taper of the descenders, but scribes soon adopted the fashion of using broken strokes wherever it was possible to use them. Once the scribes had adopted the details of the new style, the developments in this variety seem for a time to reflect those in Secretary. As in the contemporary Secretary hands scribes emphasized the various stylistic features in turn. In manuscripts produced about 1400 and in the early years of the fifteenth century there is the same emphasis upon broken strokes and horns (Plate 2 (ii)). The mid-fifteenth-century hands are compact, contain simplified forms (Plate 3 (i)), and in some cases show traces of splay.

The adoption of broken strokes and horns made some of the letter forms of the script extremely difficult to write, consequently scribes devised simpler ways of forming the most complex graphs of the script. They introduced a variant of the two-compartment **a**, based upon the Textura form. The scribe first made a single lobe, and then divided it into the two compartments by means of a short horizontal stroke (Plate 3 (i)). There is also a version based upon the 'capital' form. This is composed of a single stroke: a short loop followed by a larger loop in the reverse direction (Plate 3 (ii)). Both variants reduce the number of strokes and movements required to produce this complex graph. In the case of two-compartment **g**, the direction of the tail stroke was reversed to enable the scribe to approach the following letter without raising the pen (Plate 3 (ii)). Although the incidence of simplified forms increases as the fifteenth century progressed, their presence provides an unreliable criterion for dating, since most of them appear early in highly current hands.[2]

During the second half of the fifteenth century the principal variations which took place in the standard variety lie not so much in the morphology as in the proportions and execution of the handwriting. As scribes used Secretary more often, their habituation to the duct, letter forms, and style of calligraphy of the new script seems somehow

[1] *STC.*, 6446.

[2] For example, I have found the 'capital' **a** form and **g** with reversed tail stroke in a highly current hand in one of the King's Bench Rolls for 1386–7 (P.R.O., KB 27/502).

to have made the writing of good Anglicana more difficult. The less complicated Secretary forms of **a**, **g**, and **w** appear frequently in place of the regular Anglicana forms. The size and proportions of each individual letter seem to vary, even within a single word (Plates 3 (ii), 21 (iii)). The vertical ascenders and descenders frequently go out of the vertical, and the resulting 'splay', when compared with that of a Secretary hand, is obviously accidental. With increasing frequency the scribes abandoned any pretence at calligraphy, and the handwriting sprawls across the page (Plate 21 (iii)).

ANGLICANA FORMATA AND BASTARD ANGLICANA

Books written in Anglicana Formata and Bastard Anglicana show the details of the new style of calligraphy earlier than those written in the less formal variety, because they were usually written more meticulously (Plates 2 (i), 5 (i)). During the last quarter of the fourteenth century scribes began to form the lobes of the letters **d** and **q** by means of broken strokes, and the practice was soon extended to the formation of other letters: in particular to **a**, **c**, **g**, **o**, and even to the loops of ascenders (Plates 5 (i) and (ii)). The short **r** derived from the earlier book hands was remodelled by analogy with the Secretary form (Plate 6 (i)).

About 1400 the writing of Anglicana Formata reached a climax in the large well-spaced calligraphic hands used for the massive volumes containing vernacular texts.[1] The size of the hands enabled scribes to contain successfully those details of the new style of calligraphy which were most suited to this variety of the script. In some cases the hands are so well written that it is difficult to distinguish them from those of Bastard Anglicana. Scribes continued to use this large calligraphic version of Anglicana Formata for de luxe copies of vernacular texts until the mid fifteenth century,[2] when they began to replace it by Bastard Secretary. In the smaller vernacular manuscripts some scribes achieved a successful amalgam of Anglicana Formata and Secretary, which is almost a separate style (Plate 19 (ii)). It contains a high proportion of Secretary forms, and could be, and was written currently. The majority of manuscripts written in Anglicana Formata reveal the progressive assimilation of details from Secretary (Plate 6 (i)), and in the second half of the fifteenth century this is accompanied by a tendency to exaggerate those features of style proper to Anglicana Formata itself, such as the feet of the minims (Plate 6 (ii)). In the universities Anglicana Formata was replaced in the fifteenth century by a new kind of handwriting which it will be necessary to discuss separately later.

Bastard Anglicana was also modified under the impact of the new style of calligraphy (Plate 7 (ii)), and during the fifteenth century by the influence of Bastard Secretary (Plate 8 (i)); but since the Bastard hands were in origin a mixture, they were particularly prone to idiosyncratic variation as scribes added to the mixture or varied the proportions of the ingredients.[3] Although towards the end of the fifteenth century the writing of Bastard Secretary was disciplined by the influence of new models imported from the Continent, these models made the writing of Bastard Anglicana more difficult. As

[1] For examples see *The Ellesmere Chaucer Reproduced in Facsimile* (Manchester, 1910); Pal. Soc. i, pl. 101; and W. W. Skeat, *Twelve Facsimiles of Old English MSS.* (Oxford, 1892), pl. ix.

[2] For example, in the following manuscripts of works by Lydgate: Bodl. MSS. Digby 230, 232, and Rawl. C. 466.

[3] Further examples of idiosyncratic hands may be seen in Wright, *EVH.*, pl. 18; N. Pal. Soc. i, pl. 220.

a result it did not survive as a distinct form of writing. Its features were incorporated into the idiosyncratic attempts on the part of individual scribes to produce a calligraphic substitute for Textura (Plate 8 (ii)), and which are perhaps best described as 'Fere-textura'.

THE HANDWRITING OF UNIVERSITY SCRIBES IN THE FIFTEENTH CENTURY

In the universities, and particularly at Oxford, the scribes achieved a blend of Anglicana and Secretary which resulted in what was virtually a new kind of book hand. It replaced Anglicana Formata as the principal academic book hand in the fifteenth century, and remained in use until it was replaced in turn by the advent of the printed text.[1] The hands are small, highly current, and compact. Although highly current, this is a much more conscious style of writing than at first meets the eye. The fluency is carefully controlled, and the letter forms are consciously simplified and compressed. Although this highly distinctive style of handwriting owed much to the influence of Secretary, this influence is not immediately recognizable in the early-fifteenth-century hands (Plate 17 (i)). We can only see how much they owe to Secretary by analysing them closely, or by comparing them with French hands of a similar kind.[2] However, in hands written about the middle of the century the influence of the duct of the new script becomes more recognizable. The characteristic splay, accompanied by distinctive Secretary graphs, appears more frequently (Plate 17 (ii)), and in the 1460s and 70s the hands tend to resemble the contemporary Secretary hands more closely as other features of the new style of calligraphy emerge (Plate 18 (i)). In manuscripts produced in the last quarter of the century scribes tend to develop more personal styles. The hands are more current, and some scribes even adopted humanist forms (Plate 18 (ii)).

THE HANDWRITING OF INDIVIDUAL SCRIBES

Many fifteenth-century scribes were able to write well in more than one script (Plate 22), and manuscripts in which the scribe has used one script for the text and another for headings or commentaries are common (Plates 19 (ii), 20 (i)). However, the existence side by side of two different cursive scripts which nevertheless possessed parity of status in the hierarchy of scripts, and which shared many features of the new style of calligraphy, created a state of confusion among the scribes. As soon as there are two ways of writing the same thing, a mixture of the two is inevitable (Plate 24 (i)). The existence of separate varieties of the two scripts provided further ingredients for the mixture. In such circumstances it is easy to understand why the handwriting of foreign scribes, accustomed as they were to only one cursive script, is frequently superior to that of their English colleagues (Plate 24 (ii)).[3] By far the greater number of

[1] The type faces of early printed books were not based on this kind of handwriting, but either on Textura, or on more formal cursive models such as the more idiosyncratic Bastard Secretary hands (cf. Bodl. MS. Laud Misc. 616 with E. G. Duff, *Early English Printing* (London, 1896), no. x).

[2] e.g. *Mss. datés*, vol. i, pls. lvi (ii), lix, lxi, lxxi (ii).

[3] During the fifteenth century a number of foreign scribes worked in England for English patrons. For accounts of some of them see R. A. B. Mynors, *Catalogue of the MSS. of Balliol College, Oxford* (Oxford, 1963), pp. xxvi–xxviii, xlii, xlviii–xlix; the same writer's 'A Fifteenth-Century Scribe: T. Werken', *Transactions of the Cambridge Bibliographical Society*, i (1950), p. 97; and M. B. Parkes, 'A Fifteenth-Century Scribe: Henry Mere', *Bodleian Library Record*, vi (1961), p. 654.

manuscripts produced in England during the fifteenth century were written in hands which contain forms and features drawn from more than one script. Not all these mixed hands were produced by accident. Many scribes, particularly in the second half of the century, carefully selected features from various scripts and incorporated them into their handwriting (Plates 8 (ii), 14 (i)). The majority of mixed hands are difficult to date unless one is able to relate sufficient details of the separate ingredients to dated or datable examples of the scripts from which they were drawn (cf. Plate 24 (i)).

The impact of the new developments in the calligraphy of cursive handwriting had a profound effect upon the standard of handwriting in this country. Whereas the developments which had taken place in English handwriting at the beginning of the fourteenth century were of a practical nature, those which were introduced at the end of the century were not. The elaborate treatment of the strokes, and of subsidiary features, made the letter forms of both cursive scripts exceedingly complex, and it required a highly skilled and punctilious scribe to reproduce them well. As a result, in manuscripts produced after about 1380, one finds a few well-defined specimens of the several varieties of the two scripts executed by skilled scribes, and many inferior specimens produced by the less expert or the less patient. Many skilled scribes developed more practical hands alongside their formal models, yet based upon them: modifications designed to restore the primary requirements of simplicity and ease of manœuvre. One finds examples of scribes who wrote meticulously on the first few pages, then slid gradually into a more comfortable style of writing even changing from one script to another in the process (Plate 21). Scribal practice became progressively idiosyncratic until with the rapid development of printing handwriting ceased to be the normal means of producing books. In the sixteenth century Secretary became the principal script in use in this country (Plate 20 (ii)). Anglicana survived only in certain government offices and the law.[1]

[1] Hence the tendency from the sixteenth century onwards to refer to it as 'Court Hand' (see above, p. xvi) or 'Chancelry' (as in Baildon and de Beauchesne, op. cit.).

A NOTE ON PALAEOGRAPHICAL TERMS

MOST of the terms used in this book to describe handwriting are used in a metaphorical sense which can be readily understood. However, the following terms perhaps ought to be explained for the benefit of the student. A *script* is the model which the scribe has in his mind's eye when he writes, whereas a *hand* is what he actually puts down on the page. The *duct* of a hand is the distinctive manner in which strokes are traced upon the writing surface: it represents the combination of such factors as the angle at which the pen was held in relation to the way in which it was cut, the degree of pressure applied to it, and the direction in which it was moved. A *stroke* is a single trace made by the pen on the page; if the stroke has no sudden change of direction, it is made in a single *movement*. A *broken stroke* is made in more than one movement, the direction of the pen being changed suddenly without its being lifted from the page. A *minim stroke* is the shortest and simplest stroke: that used to form the letters **i**, **m**, **n**, **u**. An *otiose stroke* is a superfluous stroke, one which does not form part of a letter, and which does not indicate an abbreviation. *Biting* occurs when two adjacent contrary curved strokes coalesce, as when **b** is closely followed by **o**. The terms used when describing letter forms are best elucidated by examples: the letter **b** comprises a *stem* or mainstroke which rises above the general level of the other letters (*ascender*) and a *lobe* made with a curved stroke to the right of the stem; the letter **p** a *descender* and a lobe; the letter **h** an ascender and a *limb*; the letter **t** a *shaft* and a *headstroke*. The *body* of a letter form is that part which does not include an ascender or descender.

SELECT BIBLIOGRAPHY

B. BISCHOFF, 'Paläographie', *Deutsche Philologie im Aufriß* (Munich, 1952) pp. 379–451.

—— G. I. LIEFTINCK, and G. BATELLI, *Nomenclature des écritures livresques du ixe au xvie siècle* (Paris, 1954).

P. CHAPLAIS, *English Royal Documents, King John–Henry VI 1199–1461* (Oxford, 1971).

E. CROUS and J. KIRCHNER, *Die gotischen Schriftarten* (Leipzig, 1928).

H. DELITZSCH, *Geschichte der abendländischen Schreibschriftformen* (Leipzig, 1933).

N. DENHOLM-YOUNG, *Handwriting in England and Wales* (Cardiff, 1964).

J. DESTREZ, *La Pecia dans les manuscrits universitaires du xiiie et du xive siècle* (Paris, 1935).

A. I. DOYLE and M. B. PARKES, 'The Production of Copies of the *Canterbury Tales* and the *Confessio Amantis* in the Early Fifteenth Century', *Medieval Scribes, Manuscripts & Libraries: Essays Presented to N. R. Ker*, ed. M. B. PARKES and A. G. WATSON (London, 1978), pp. 163–210.

W. W. GREG, *Facsimiles of Twelve Early English MSS. in the Library of Trinity College, Cambridge* (Oxford, 1913).

H. E. P. GRIEVE, *Some Examples of English Handwriting* (Chelmsford, 1949).

—— *More Examples of English Handwriting* (Chelmsford, 1950).

L. C. HECTOR, *The Handwriting of English Documents* (London, 1966).

R. W. HUNT, 'Palaeography', *Chambers's Encyclopaedia*, x (London, 1950).

H. JENKINSON, *The Later Court Hands in England from the 15th to the 17th Century* (Cambridge, 1927).

C. JOHNSON and H. JENKINSON, *English Court Hand A.D. 1066–1500* (Oxford, 1915).

E. JOHNSTON, *Writing and Illuminating, and Lettering* (London, 1962).

N. R. KER, 'Eton College MS 44 and its Exemplar', *Varia Codicologica: Essays Presented to G. I. Lieftinck*, i, Litterae textuales (1972), 48–60.

J. KIRCHNER, *Scriptura Gothica Libraria* (Munich, 1966).

E. A. LOWE, 'Handwriting' in *The Legacy of the Middle Ages*, ed. C. G. CRUMP and E. F. JACOB (Oxford, 1926).

C. T. MARTIN, *Wright's Court Hand Restored*, ed. C. T. MARTIN (London, 1879).

New Palaeographical Society, *Facsimiles of Ancient Manuscripts &c.*, ed. E. M. THOMPSON, G. F. WARNER, F. G. KENYON, and J. P. GILSON, 1st series (London, 1903–12); 2nd series (London, 1913–30).

Palaeographical Society, *Facsimiles of Manuscripts and Inscriptions*, ed. E. A. BOND, E. M. THOMPSON, and G. F. WARNER, 1st series (London, 1873–83); 2nd series (London, 1884–94).

E. POULLE, *Paléographie des écritures cursives en France du xve au xviie siècle* (Geneva, 1966).

M. PROU, *Manuel de paléographie latine et française* (Paris, 1924).

C. SAMARAN and R. MARICHAL, *Catalogue des manuscrits en écriture latine, portant des indications de date de lieu ou de copiste* (Paris, 1959–).

W. W. SKEAT, *Twelve Facsimiles of Old English Manuscripts* (Oxford, 1892).

F. STEFFENS, *Lateinische Paläographie* (Berlin and Leipzig, 1929).

E. M. THOMPSON, *An Introduction to Greek and Latin Palaeography* (Oxford, 1912).

S. H. THOMSON, *Latin Book Hands of the later Middle Ages 1100–1500* (Cambridge, 1969).

A. G. WATSON, *Catalogue of Dated and Datable Manuscripts c. 700–1600 in the Department of Manuscripts, the British Library* (London, 1979).

C. E. WRIGHT, *English Vernacular Hands from the Twelfth to the Fifteenth Centuries* (Oxford, 1960).

A NOTE ON THE TRANSCRIPTIONS

A TRANSCRIPTION is not an edition. The object of a transcription is to indicate clearly to the reader what can be seen in the manuscript, what parts of the text have been corrected, inserted, lost, or damaged, and how the text has been laid out on the page. However, it is impossible to record precisely in print all the variations that can be found in script. This applies particularly to variations in spacing. In the transcriptions I have regularized the spacing of the manuscripts according to modern principles, but I have retained the original punctuation and 'capital' letters, even when the scribes use 'capitals' in an erratic way.

I have observed the following conventions:

In transcriptions of verse texts I have preserved the lineation of the manuscript. In transcriptions of prose texts I have indicated the end of each line in the manuscript by means of a vertical stroke |.

Rubrics and headings have been printed in bold face type.

In transcriptions of English texts þ^{t} and w^{t} have been retained, and the Tironian sign for 'et' has been indicated by means of ⁊, because it is not always possible to determine how they should be expanded. Where the sign ꝭ occurs as a grammatical sign to indicate the plural or the genitive case, and it has not been possible to determine the spelling from forms written out in full elsewhere in the text, I have left it as it stands. I have expanded all other abbreviations in accordance with the spelling used by the scribe elsewhere in the manuscript. Where **þ** is indistinguishable from **y**, I have printed **y**.

In transcriptions of vernacular texts all expanded abbreviations have been printed in italics. In transcriptions of Latin texts, since Latin orthography is more stable, I have expanded all abbreviations silently.

I have preserved the distinction in the manuscripts between **u** and **v** since this is a feature of spelling, but I have not preserved the distinction between **i** and **j** since until about 1500 the two appear to be calligraphic variants. I have transcribed **j** throughout as **i**.

I have used the following symbols:

⌜ ⌝ enclose words and letters which have been inserted by the scribe either between the lines, or in the margin.

[ ] enclose words and letters which have been deleted by the scribe by means of crossing out, erasure, or expunctuation.

〈 〉 enclose letters which have been supplied in the transcription where the manuscript is deficient through damage, or where letters have been hidden by the binding. Where traces of the letter are still visible in the manuscript, the supplied letter has been printed in roman type. Where no traces of the letter remain, the supplied letter has been printed in italics. Where it has not been possible to determine the nature of the missing letters from the context, dots have been supplied to indicate the number of letters which would fit into the space available.

( ) enclose letters which have been supplied either where the scribe has omitted them by mistake, or where he has omitted them on purpose but has failed to use the appropriate mark of abbreviation. They also enclose insertions of my own.[1]

¶ has been used to indicate any form of paragraph mark used by the rubricator.

In fifteenth-century manuscripts containing English texts, some letters are often furnished with additional strokes which in a Latin text would indicate an abbreviation, but which may or may not do so in English. For example, compare Plate 12 (ii), 5 'angur' with Plate 2 (ii), 10 'multiplicar*e*'; Plate 12 (ii), 5 'and' with Plate 22 (i), 25 'abstinend*um*'; and Plate 3 (ii), 11 'all' with Plate 11 (i), 9 'al*iter*'.

There are two reasons why the interpretation of these strokes is difficult. The first is that the spelling of English, especially of the ends of words which often involved, or could involve, inflexions, was less stable than that of Latin. It is therefore easier to tell in Latin whether or not a word is complete. The stroke which descends from the **d** in Plate 15 (i), 10 'quod' must be an otiose stroke, whereas that in Plate 22 (i), 25 'abstinend*um*' must be a mark of suspension. The second reason is that the fifteenth-century scribes used otiose strokes as a feature of calligraphic decoration, and some of these strokes can look very much like marks of abbreviation. In the more carefully written hands most of the otiose strokes were traced as hairlines (Plates 6 (ii), 14 (ii)), and it is less difficult to interpret the intention of the scribe. But in many current hands, particularly in the latter part of the fifteenth century (Plates 3 (ii) and 12 (ii)), the scribes retain the otiosa, and what appears as a hairline in a calligraphic hand often appears as a firm stroke in a more current one (compare Plate 12 (ii), 7 'if' with Plate 6 (ii), a, 12 and 15 'of').

When such strokes occur in the middle of a word it is usually possible to tell whether or not the word is complete. In Plate 12 (ii), 4 there is a stroke over 'ght' in the word 'doughter', but there can be no question of a contraction at this point, whereas in Plate 19 (ii), 6 'ouercu*m*mys' the stroke over the vowel indicates the omission of 'm'. In the case of otiose strokes which occur in the middle of a word, I have drawn attention to their existence in the notes, but I have ignored them in the transcriptions.[2]

The problem of interpretation is more acute when the strokes are added to final letters, where they might indicate the suspension of final -e, endings like -es or -is/ys, or occasionally -m or -n. In Plate 3 (ii), 5 the scribe has added a stroke to the 'g' in 'yong'. If he had scanned the line:

To whóm on knées two yóng-e fólk-e críde

then the stroke would indicate the omission of the final -e required by the metre. However, he might have scanned the line:

To whóm on kné-es twó yong fólk-e críde

in which case final -e would not be required, and the stroke would be otiose.[3] For a further example see the note to Plate 12 (ii), 20 'good'. The scribes frequently made the

[1] This symbol cannot be used for this purpose when transcribing manuscripts produced in England in the sixteenth century, since it is then used by scribes to indicate a parenthesis. The earliest dated example I have is the Wells Psalter written by Peter Meghen in 1514. I suggest that when round brackets are used by the scribe the transcriber should use italicized square brackets to indicate his own insertions.

[2] On the problem of '-cion' or '-cioun', see note to Plate 6 (ii).

[3] Some of the other manuscripts read 'yonge folkes', others read 'yong folk ther'.

strokes in different ways according to the letter they accompany and not according to the nature of a possible suspension: see Plate 3 (ii), and note. A satisfactory interpretation of such strokes is not possible without a detailed study of the language of the manuscript. This is possible only in an edition, although even there the presence of such strokes and the situations in which they occur should not pass unnoticed. In a transcription it is not safe either to ignore them, or to treat them as marks of abbreviation. I have therefore indicated them by means of an apostrophe.

LIST OF PLATES

17 (i) Cambridge: University Library, MS. Ff. 3. 27, fol. 45^r.
(ii) Oxford: Bodleian Library, MS. Bodley 52, fol. 151^r.

18 (i) Oxford: New College, MS. 305, fol. 104^r.
(ii) Oxford: University College, MS. 156, fol. 1^r.

19 (i) Cambridge: Gonville and Caius College, MS. 282/675, fol. 25^r.
(ii) Oxford: Bodleian Library, MS. Bodley 467, fol. 120^r.

20 (i) Oxford: Bodleian Library, MS. Bodley 248, fol. 100^r.
(ii) Oxford: Bodleian Library, MS. Bodley 431, fol. 96^r.

21 London: Society of Antiquaries, MS. 223, fols. 1^v, 2^v, and 30^v.

22 (i) Shrewsbury School, MS. viii, fol. 82^v.
(ii) Glasgow: University Library, Hunterian MS. U. 5. 3, fol. 41^r.

23 (i) Worcester: Cathedral Muniments, Account Roll, C222.
(ii) Oxford: Bodleian Library, MS. Hatton 11, fol. 90^r.

24 (i) Oxford: Magdalen College, MS. Lat. 154, fol. 30^r, col. b.
(ii) Oxford: Balliol College, MS. 30, fol. 119^v, col. b.

Photographs are reproduced here by kind permission of the following: His Grace, the Archbishop of Canterbury and the Trustees of Lambeth Palace Library; the President and Council of the Society of Antiquaries of London; the Master and Fellows of Balliol College, Oxford; the Curators of the Bodleian Library, Oxford; the British Library Board; the Syndics of the University Library, Cambridge; the President and Fellows of Corpus Christi College, Oxford; the Librarian of the University of Glasgow; the Master and Fellows of Gonville and Caius College, Cambridge; the President and Fellows of Magdalen College, Oxford; the Warden and Fellows of Merton College, Oxford; the Warden and Fellows of New College, Oxford; the Governors of Shrewsbury School; the Master and Fellows of Trinity College, Cambridge; the Master and Fellows of University College, Oxford; the Dean and Chapter of Worcester.

THE PLATES

1

84 p 171

huiusmodi excommunicacionum suspensionum et interdicti sentencias nullas esse decernimus ipso iure prelatus et qui huiusmodi sequestraciones fecerit quousque eas revocaverit ipso facto a pontificalibus sit suspensus. De oblacionibus capellarum restituendis

Gracia que de concedentis benignitate procedit recipiente [illegible] ecclesie manifeste reddit ingratum si vertitur in abusum et eius non contenta finibus extenditur in alterius lesionem. Ecclesia quidem prudencie pietatis dum alteri pro altero non multo incommodo condicionem asserit si quando parochiana persona capellam propriam desiderat optinere idque causa iusta mediante concesserit semper advertere consuevit ut id fiat sine suo preiudicio alieno. Quod et nos salubri et optimo remedio prosequentes statuimus et districte precipimus ut capellani ministrantes in capellis huiusmodi que aliis sue matricis ecclesie sunt concesse universas oblaciones et alia que ipsi non perciperent ad matricem ecclesiam pertinere iure deberent eius rectori sine difficultate restituant. ad id tamquam alienum iuste nequeant detinere. [illegible] restitucionis contempserint suspensionis vinculo quousque restituerint se noverint innodatum. De domibus ecclesiarum

urbanarum quondam antiquarum persone cum ecclesiis suis [illegible] reficiendis. Et ecclesias [illegible] multa bona recipiunt domos ipsarum et certa edificia negligunt ita ut [illegible] non conveniant et diruta non restaurent. propter quod ipsarum ecclesiarum status deformitatis occumbit et multa incommoda subsequuntur. decernimus atque precipimus ut commissi [illegible] domos et c.

Icest oreysoun envea nostre dame seinte Marie a seint [illegible] de Parys, e lui comanda quil le apreist al pueple, e qui chescun iour en bon devocion le dirra, homme en le siecle ne avera, ne del enemy engyne serra, ne passioun en terre soffrera, ne femme denfaunt perera, ne mort soudeyne ne avendra, ne desconfes murra.

Gloriouse dame que le fiz dieu portastes, e a tel benneure portiure sanz compaignie de homme concevistes, dame dolouse e saunz [illegible] virgine de le fiz dieu enfauntastes, e de vostre virginal let virginalment le letastes. Dame si verroiement come cest voirs e ie fermement le crei, eiez en garde la alme e le cors de moy. E pur celes nounddisables ioies que le fiz dieu e le vostre fist quant il releva de mort e verablement a vous apparust, e que aviez quant il mounta en ciel veiaunt vos eux, e que aviez quant il vous vint tot festinaunz come [illegible] ou sa court tote celestre, e vous assist al destre de lui e vous corona reigne de ciel e de terre, pur

PLATES 1–3. Anglicana Book Hands

1 (i). End of the thirteenth century. Oxford: University College, MS. 148, fol. 84^{r}.

Canons of the Legatine council held at London in April 1268, usually known as the 'Constitutiones' of Cardinal Ottobuono; now forming part (fols. 71–89) of the memorandum book of John Croucher, Dean of Chichester 1426–47 (*v.* W. D. Pecham, 'Dean Croucher's Book', *Sussex Archaeological Collections*, lxxxiv (1945), p. 11). Text of the Canons ed. F. M. Powicke and C. R. Cheney, *Councils and Synods with other Documents relating to the English Church* (Oxford, 1964), ii, p. 747, where this manuscript is designated as C. Text of this plate, ibid., ii, p. 766.

Written towards the end of the thirteenth century (cf. *ECH.*, pl. xvii, b, dated 1272).

Typical example of Anglicana found in books of this kind at this period. Note the characteristic letter forms of the script (*v.* p. xiv). Headings are in the smaller 'gothic' book hand. Features characteristic of hands of this period include: headstroke of **a** not always closed up to form the top lobe of the two-compartment form (12, 'ecclesiam'); **r** has a pronounced shoulder stroke (2, 'reuocauerit'); the elaborate forked ascenders of **b**, **h**, **k**, and **l**, in which the forks are 'looped back'. The loop to the right of the ascender, formed by the approach stroke, became progressively larger during the course of the second half of the century. The broad headstroke of **a** (7, 'persona'), the heavy diagonal of the looped ascender of **d** (6, 'prouidencie'), and the broad strokes forming the marks of abbreviation (1, 'suspensionum', 'interdicti'), indicate that the pen was held or cut at a very oblique angle.

huiusmodi excommunicationum suspensionum et interdicti sententias nullas esse decernimus ipso iure. | Prelatus eciam qui huiusmodi sequestrationes fecerit quousque eas reuocauerit ipso facto | a pontificalibus sit suspensus.

De oblacionibus capellarum restituendis | Matrici ecclesie. Gracia que de concedentis benignitate procedit recipientem | manifeste reddit ingratum si vertitur in abusum. et suis non contenta | f⟨*i*⟩nibus extenditur in alterius lesionem. Ecclesiastice quidem prouidencie pietas dum | alteri per alterum non uult iniquam (*for* nunquam) conditionem afferri si quando priuata persona capel-|lam propriam desiderat optinere. idque causa iusta mediante concesserit semper adi-|cere consueuit. vt id fiat sine Iuris preiudicio alieni. Quod et nos salubri et | oportuno remedio prosequentes statuimus et districte precipimus vt capellani | ministrantes in capellis huiusmodi que saluo Iure matricis ecclesie sunt concesse | vniuersas oblationes et cetera que ipsis non recipientibus ad matricem ecclesiam perue-|nire deberent ipsius rectori sine difficultate restituant. cum id tanquam alie-|num iuste nequeant detinere. Si quis autem restituere contempserit.· sus-|pensionis vinculo quousque restituerit se nouerit innodatum.

De domibus ecclesia|rum reficiendis. Inprobam quorundam auariciam persequentes qui cum ecclesiis suis | et ecclesiasticis beneficiis multa bona percipiunt domos ipsarum et cetera edificia | negligunt ita vt integra non conseruent et dirupta non restaurent. propter | quod ipsarum ecclesiarum statum deformitas occupat et multa incommoda subsequntur. | statuimus atque precipimus vt vniuersi clerici suorum beneficiorum domos et cetera.

(ii). c. 1340–50. London: British Museum, MS. Harley 2253, fol. 134^{v}.

Prose version of 'Les cinqs joies de Nostre Dame', here attributed to Maurice de Sully, Bishop of Paris (d. 1196) (*v.* P. Meyer, *Romania*, xv, p. 307; E. Stengel, *Codex Digby 86* (1871), p. 6; N. R. Ker, *Facsimile of British Museum MS. Harley 2253*, E.E.T.S. (o.s.), 255, p. xv, item 104).

Written *c.* 1340–50 (*v.* Ker, op. cit., p. xxi).

The bulk of the manuscript was written in a somewhat half-hearted attempt to produce Anglicana Formata, mainly by adding feet to the minims, but in some of the prose texts, as here, the scribe reverts to the less formal variety of the script.

Compare with the previous plate and note here the change in the angle at which the pen was held or cut, resulting in broader vertical strokes. The elaborate forked ascenders have been abandoned, and the approach stroke to the right of the ascender has been developed into a pronounced hook. For the most part **r** has lost its shoulder stroke (1, 'oreysoun', but cf. 1, 'Moris'). The limb of **h** regularly descends below the line of writing (7, 'homme'). The rounded **w** (11, 'vewablement') is prominent at this date, but is found as late as the fifteenth century. The **g** form (8, 'virginalement') is unusual. **a** is always a two-compartment form.

The scribe distinguishes between the less formal Anglicana used for the text of the book and that used for the documents (Ker, op. cit., fols. 1^{v}, 142). In the book he writes a slightly larger hand, and omits certain current features such as the connecting strokes between the descenders and the headstrokes of **f** and **s**.

On the problems to be encountered when transcribing French vernacular manuscripts produced in England *v.* F. W. Maitland's introduction to *Year Books of Edward II*, i, Selden Soc. xvii (1903), pp. xxxix ff.

¶ Icest oreysoun enueia n*ostr*e dame seinte Marie a seint Moris euesque | de parys/ e ly comanda quil le ap*ri*st al pueple/ e qui chescun iour | ou bon deuocion le dirra hounte en le siecle ne auera/ ne del enymy | engyne serra/ ne passioun en terre soffrera/ ne femme denfant periera/| ne mesauenture ne auendra/ ne desconfes murra.

¶ Gloriouse dame que le fitz dieu portastes/ e a ta benure porture sanz | conysaunce de houme concustes / sauntz dolour e sauue ta v*ir*gine|te le fitz dieu enfauntastes/ e de v*ir*ginal let v*ir*ginalment le letastes | dame si veroiement come cest voirs e ie fermement le croy/ eyez en | garde lalme e le cors de moy/ E pur celes noundisables ioyes que le | fitz dieu e le v*ostre* v*ous* fist/ q*ua*nt il releua de mort e vewablement a vous | apparust/ e que auyez q*ua*nt il mounta en ciel. veaunt vos eux/ e que | auyez q*ua*nt vynt tot festinauntz count*re* v*ous* ou la court tote celestre/ | si v*ous* assist al destre de ly/ e v*ous* corona reigne de cel e de terre/ pur |

2 (i). 1381. Oxford: Bodleian Library, MS. Douce 257 (*SC.* 21831), fol. 38^{r}.

Alexander de Villa Dei, 'Massa Compoti' (Thorndike and Kibre, 1557, *v.* Sarton, ii (1931), p. 617), with commentary possibly by Simon Bredon (Thorndike and Kibre, 1085. On Bredon *v.* Emden, *BRUO.*; and R. T. Gunther, *Early Science in Oxford,* ii, O.H.S. lxxviii (1923), p. 52.). The text of the poem ed. R. Steele, *Opera hactenus inedita Rogeri Baconi*, Fasc. vi (1926), p. 268; text of lines 1–8 of this plate from lines 198–205 of the poem.

Written in 1381 (fol. 62^{v}, 'Explicit massa compoti Anno Domini $M^{lo}CCC^{mo}$ Octogesimo primo ipso die felicis et andacti', i.e. 30 August 1381).

The scribe has copied the text of the poem (lines 1–8) in Anglicana Formata, and the commentary (9–20) in the less formal variety of the script. Note the difference in the size of the two kinds of handwriting, and in the formation of the minim strokes. In the hand used for the text the letter **a** does not extend so far above the general level of the other letters as it does in the commentary (1, 'anno', cf. 14, 'alius'); the back of **d** is more upright (2, 'due', cf. 9, 'de'); the shaft of **t** protrudes above the headstroke, whereas in the commentary it does not (4, 'tibi', cf. 9, 'autor'); and the form of short-**s** is different from that used in the commentary (1, 'decies', cf. 9, 'concurrens'). In the hand used for the commentary the duct of the handwriting is more fluent; ascenders and descenders are longer in relation to the size of the body of the letter forms. The cursive form of **e** appears in the commentary (12, 'concurrens'), but not in the text.

Compare with the previous plate and note developments which had taken place in this variety: the changes in the shapes of **r** and **s** (9, 'concurrens'), in the treatment of the ascenders, and in the more fluent handling of the minim strokes.

The influence of the new style of calligraphy associated with the recently introduced Secretary script is more obvious in the Anglicana Formata, particularly in the lobes of the letters **d** and **q** (2, 'due', 'quas').

(E)bdomode decies quini numera(n)tur in anno.
Atque due post quas lux vna dueve supersunt
Anno bisexti. superesse duas tibi scito.
Ex his augmentis concurrentes tibi fiant
Addendo semper vnum formabis in anno.
Bisexti. binos iungas numero preeunti.
Quod superat 7 retine septemque iacendo.
Per concurrentes curres annis quater apta.

// Hic agit autor de (con)currentibus. Vnde concurrens | est numerus non excedens septenarium qui simul | iunctus cum regulari feriali sit quota feria men|sis quilibet incipiat et ideo dicitur concurrens a con | quod est simul et a currens quasi simul currens cum re|gulari et dicitur alius numerus regularis quia cum (con)curren|te regulariter primam feriam mensis ostendit Prouenit | autem concurrens ex superhabundancia vnius diei in | anno communi et ex superhabundancia duorum dierum in | anno bisextili supra in quinquaginta duas | ebdomodas que sunt in anno et quia ante finem | anni non accidit tale crementum super integras |

(ii). 1419. Cambridge: Trinity College, MS. O. 1. 31 (James, 1055), fol. 16^{v}.

Alexander de Villa Dei, 'Carmen de Algorismo' (Thorndike and Kibre, 597) with commentary (Thorndike and Kibre, 791; *v.* Sarton, ii (1931), p. 616). The text of the poem has been printed by J. O. Halliwell, *Rara Mathematica* (1841), p. 73.

Written in 1419 (col. 45^{v}, 'Explicit quod J. B. . . . Anno Domini 1419 . . . ', cf. also fol. 18^{v}).

Unlike the scribe of the previous plate, the scribe here has used the less formal variety of Anglicana for both text and commentary. Compare with the hand used for the commentary in the previous plate and note here the increased influence of Secretary: the change in the direction of the minim strokes; the use of broken strokes in the formation of **g** (3, 'digito') and **o** (12, 'maior'), the stems of **c** and **e** (20, 'precedentem'), as well as in the lobes of the letters **d** and **q**; the slope of the descenders; and the appearance of horns, especially on the top of **e** (14, 'ducenda'). The resulting 'prickly' appearance is characteristic of hands of this period, both Anglicana and Secretary (cf. Pl. 11 (ii)). Note that the shaft of the letter **t** now protrudes above the headstroke in this variety of the script (1, 'ante').

Note the drastic abbreviation of technical terms which would appear frequently in a text of this nature: e.g. 1, 'numerus', 16, 'productus', and 24, 'linea'.

For a well-written document hand of this period *v.* Pl. 23 (i).

.versus. Si nichil in fine remanet numerus datus ante
Est cubicus cubicam radicem subtripla prebent
Cum digito iuncto quem sub prima posuisti
Hec cubice ducta numerum reddent tibi primum
Si quid erit remanens non est cubicus set habetur
Maior sub primo qui constat radix cubicati
Seruarique docet quicquid radice remansit
Extracto numero decet hec addi cubicato
Quo facto numerus reddi debet tibi primus
Nam debes per se radicem multiplicare
Exhinc in numerum duces quo prouenit inde
Sub primo cubicus maior sic inuenietur
Illi iungatur remanens et primus habetur

Hic docet auctor quod si nichil remanet radix/ ducenda est in se | .bis. et producit numerum primo propositum/ qui fuit numerus cubicus/ set si ali|quid fuerit residuum numerus productus non fuit cubicus. set radix in | se ductus cubice producti maximum cubicum sub numero proposito contentum/ | cui si addideris illud quod remansit/ habebis numerum primo propositum/ | $.ii^{a}$. Set quia difficile est scire sine multiplicacione quod numerus resultat ex ductu di-|giti in se cubice/ Ideo composui precedentem figuram per quam ille | faciliter potest scribi in concursu .ii. litterarum radices continencium appare-|bit summa quesita/ per eandem eciam figuram potest haberi numerus resultans | ex ductu in se per alium ut bis .2. ter uel ex ductu in alium per primum | ut .bis. ter. bis. sumenda est radix in linea descendente ex parte | sinistra/ et alius numerus in qua radix ducitur [sumendus] sumendus |

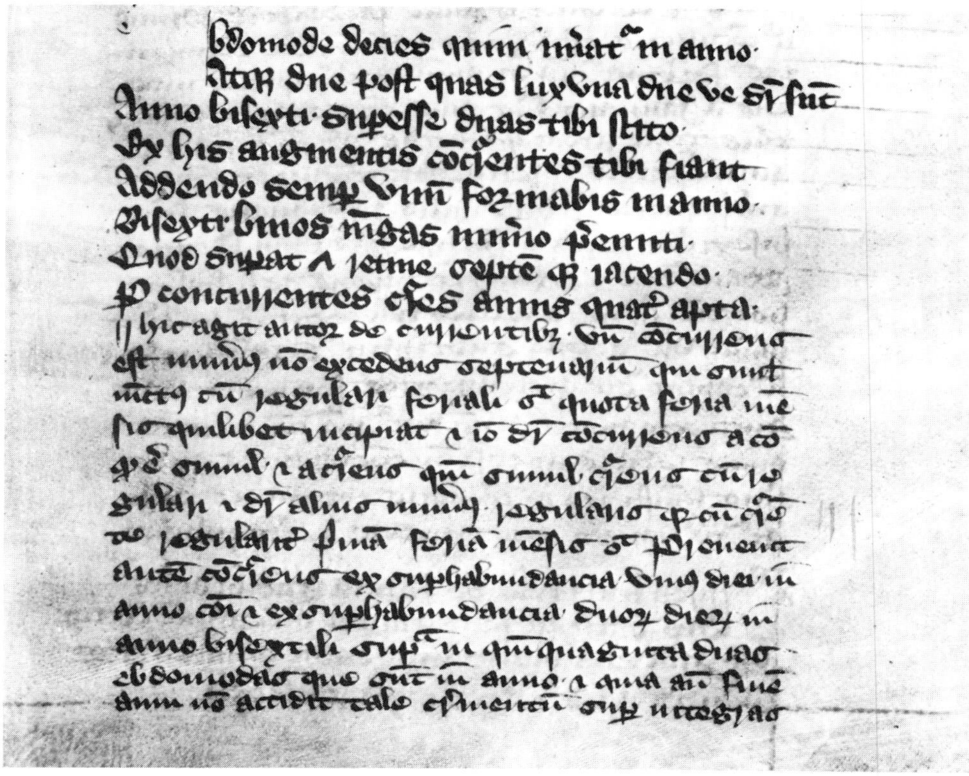

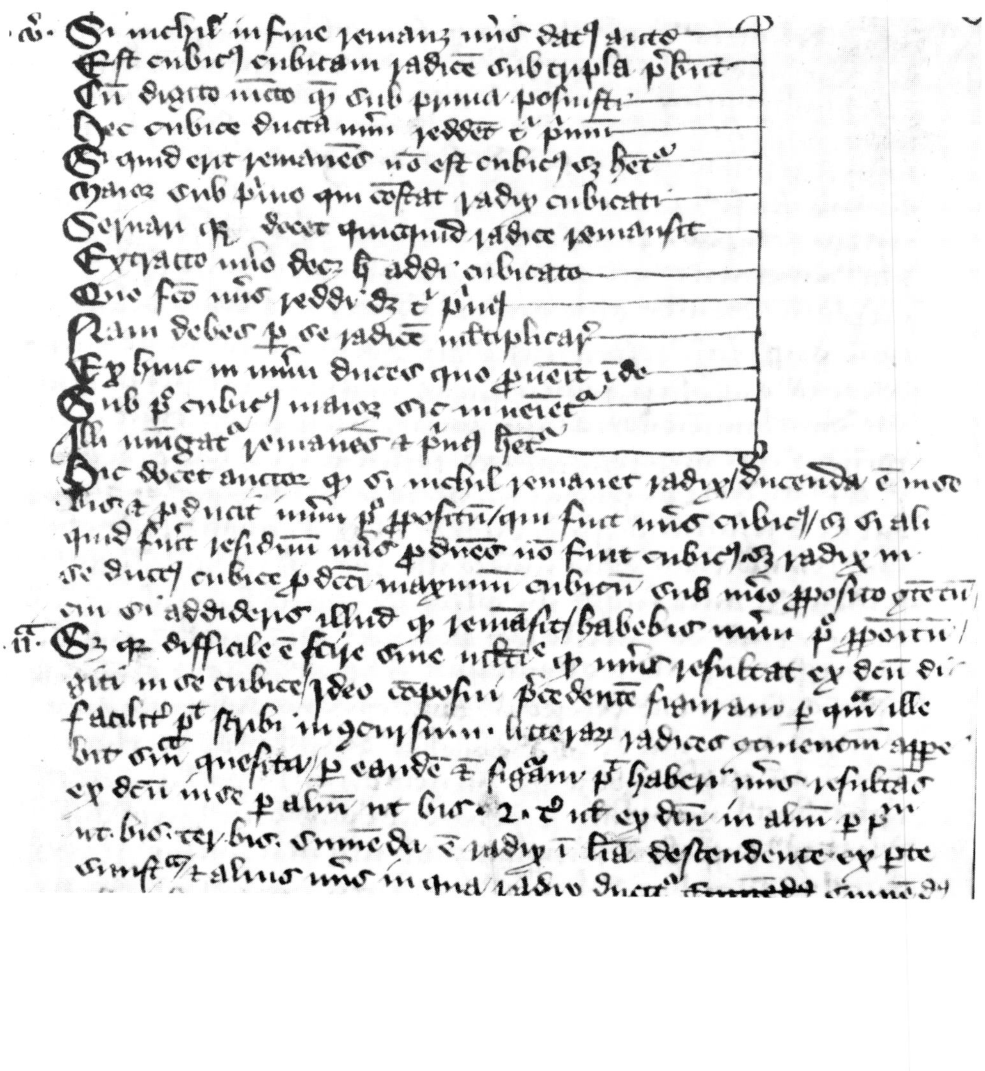

3

spicam celticam et saluncam quia montana est et spica celtica alia spice nardi et alba est et in septentrionali plaga reperitur et pro ea ponitur salunca. Spica nardi quo magis est et terrea non debet poni in medicinis. Spica nardi habet virtutem confortandi ex aromaticitate sua et ponticitate sua dissolvit et ex qualitatibus suis et amaritudinis. Contra sincopim et cardiacam passionem sumphebitur cum pulvere ex aqua rosarum decoctionis eius vel ex tali aqua et zucara fiat sirupus. Contra debilitatem cerebri applicetur naribus. Contra reuma frigidum pulvis spice decoquatur in oleo muscelino vel saltem communi et cum digito naribus imponatur. Talo cum oleo multum confert surditati ex causa frigida et contra putrefactionem aurium post apiata. Contra frigiditatem et indigestionem et opilationem splenis et epatis ex frigidis humoribus detur cum vino decoctionis spice. Contra putredinem gingivarum pulvis eius superponatur. Ad menstrua provocanda et matricem mundificandam et conceptum inducendum pulvis eius in sacco lineo formato ad modum digiti ponatur et sic dum bulliat in oleo muscel. vel saltem communi et postea mulier sibi supponat. Contra tenasmon ex frigida causa pulvis eius cum bombace vel extremis supponatur. Oleum quod fit de

The place yaf a thowsand savours sote
And Bachus god of wyn sate hyr beside
And Ceres next that doth of hunger bote
And as I said amyddes lay Cupide
To whom on knees two yong folke cryde
To been hir helpe but thus I lete hir lie
And ferther in the temple I gan espie

That in despite of Diane the chaste
Full many a bowe broke honge on the wall
Of maydenys suche as gonne her tymes waste
In her servise and paynted over all
Of many a story of which I touche shall
A fewe as of Calixte and Athalante
And many a mayde of which the name I wante

Semyramus Candace and Hercules
Biblis Dido Thesbe and Piramus
Tristram Isaude Paris and Achilles
Eleyne Cleopatre and Troylus
Silla and eke the mother of Romulus
All these were paynted on that other side
And all her love and in what plite they dide

3 (i). Mid fifteenth century. Oxford: Bodleian Library, MS. Wood Empt. 15 (*SC.* 8603), fol. 106^{r}.

'Liber de simplicibus medicinis' (Thorndike and Kibre, 211) usually known as the 'Circa instans' (*v.* Sarton, ii (1931), p. 241). The text is embodied in L. Thorndike, *The Herbal of Rufinus* (Chicago, 1945).

Written at Exeter by J. Bobych towards the end of the second quarter of the fifteenth century (fol. 116^{v}, 'Explicit tractatus quidam Phisice scriptus Exon' per manus J. Bobych'). According to an inscription on fol. v^{v} the book was subsequently given to the Cathedral Library at Exeter by the executors of John Snetisham who died in 1448 (*v.* Emden *BRUO.*).

Secretary influence is even stronger than in the hand of the previous plate. In addition to the use of broken strokes in the formation of the letters **a** (9, 'decoquatur'), **g** (8, 'frigidum'), and **o** (16, 'oleo'), ascenders frequently have the small rounded loops characteristic of the contemporary Secretary hands (cf. 1, 'celtica' with 4, 'habet', and compare with Pls. 10 (ii); 12 (i)). However, the slender upright shafts and descenders of **f** and long-**s** show no trace of Secretary influence. Since the letter **a** has become more complex with the introduction of broken strokes into the lobes of the letter, it extends further above the general level of the other letters (3, 'nardi'). The scribe has occasionally introduced a simplified version of the letter based upon the textura form (17, 'thenasmon').

Proportions and spacing of the hand are particularly characteristic of this period. Ascenders and descenders are longer in relation to the body of the letters, and consequently there is greater space between the lines than in earlier hands. Note also the firm sweeping approach strokes (most obvious on **v** and the et sign), and the treatment of the descending limb of **h**, which extend into this space. The shaft of **t** extends still further above the headstroke (9, 'saltem').

Note the drastic abbreviation of technical terms which would appear frequently in such a text: e.g. 4, 'aromaticitate', 5, 'diuretica', 11, 'apostemata', 12, 'humoribus'. The mark of abbreviation which appears over 11, 'apostemata' is common in manuscripts produced in the mid fifteenth century.

spicam celticam esse saliuncam qui menciuntur Est autem spica celtica similis | spice nardi Set alba est et in septentrionali plaga reperitur et pro ea ponitur | saliunca Spica nardi que nigra est vel terrea non debet poni in me-|dicinis Spica nardi habet virtutem confortandi ex aromaticitate sua et pon-|ticitate sua diuretica est ex qualitatibus suis et amaritudine Contra sin-|copin et cardiacam passionem limphetur vinum pacientis ex aqua rosarum | decoccionis eius vel ex tali aqua et zuccura fiat sirupus Contra debi-|litatem cerebri applicetur naribus. Contra reuma frigidum puluis spi-|ce decoquatur in oleo muscelino vel saltem communi et cum digito naribus | inponatur Tale eciam oleum multum confert surditati ex causa frigida | et contra putredinem aurium post apostemata Contra frigiditatem et indiges-|tionem et opilacionem splenis et epatis ex frigidis humoribus detur vinum | decoccionis spice Contra putredinem gingiuarum puluis eius super-|ponatur. Ad menstrua prouocanda et matricem mundificandam et conceptum | iuuandum Puluis eius in sacco lineo formato admodum digiti ponatur | et sic diu bulliat in oleo muscelino vel saltem communi et postea mulier | sibi supponat Contra thenasmon ex frigida causa puluis eius | cum bombace ano exterius existente superponatur Oleum quod fit de |

(ii). Last quarter of the fifteenth century. Oxford: Bodleian Library, MS. Digby 181, fol. 47^{r}.

Geoffrey Chaucer, 'The Parlement of Foules', and other poems by Chaucer and Lydgate (*v.* Hammond (1908), p. 339. The manuscript has also been described, with facsimile, by R. K. Root, *The Manuscripts of Chaucer's Troilus* (London, Chaucer Soc., 1914), p. 9). The text of this plate from 'Parlement of Foules', lines 274–94.

Written probably in the last quarter of the fifteenth century (cf. *LCH.*, pl. XLI, vi, dated 1484; and vii, dated 1497).

Despite the compactness of this hand, there is a general impression of irregularity. Upright strokes of ascenders and descenders are not always vertical. Letters like **a** and **h** vary in size even within a single word (15, 'Candace', 14, 'which'). Hooks of ascenders are at an acute angle, trail into the body of the letters (2, 'hire'), and vary considerably in size. Descenders are longer than ascenders, and frequently trail into the letters in the line below. Note simplified form of **a** based on the 'capital' form (2, 'sate'), *v.* above, p. xxii; and shaft of **t** protruding a long way above the headstroke (3, 'bote'). Note also the appearance of the less complex Secretary forms of **a** and **w** (1, 'thowsand'), and the simplified ascender of **d** alongside the looped ascender proper to the Anglicana script (2, 'god', cf. 'beside').

Note the frequency of the otiose strokes, discussed above, p. xxix. Note particularly how the scribe makes the strokes in different ways according to the letter which they accompany; cf. the strokes through ascenders of **ll** (20, 'all') and **h** (14, 'which'), and the strokes which follow **m** and **n** (5, 'whom on'), **d** (4, 'said'), and **g** (5, 'yong') (cf. also Pls. 12 (ii); 14 (ii); and 19 (ii)).

¶ The place yaf a thowsand' savours sote
and bachus god of wyn' sate hire beside
and Ceres next that doth' of hunger bote
and as I said' amyddes lay Cupide
To whom' on' knees two yong' folke cride
To been' hir helpe but thus I lete here lie
and Further in the Temple I gan' espie

¶ That in despite of Diane the Chast
Full' many a bowe broke/ hynge on the wall'
Of maydenys/ suche as gonne here tymes wast
In here *ser*uise/ and paynted' ouer all'
Of many a story of which I towche shall'
a Fewe/ as of Calixte/ and athalante
and many a maide of which' the name I wante/

¶ Semiramus Candace and hercules.
Bliblis Dido Tesbe and Piramus
Tristram Isaud Paris and achilles
Eleyne Cleopatre and Troyles
Silla and eke the mother of Romulus
all' thise were paynted' on þat othir side
and all' here love/ and in what plite they dide/

PLATES 4–6. Anglicana Formata

4 (i). 1291. Oxford: Bodleian Library, MS. Bodley 406 (*SC.* 2297), fol. 125^{v}.

'Liber sermonum de temporali'.

Written in 1291 (fol. 197^{v} 'Explicit liber iste scriptus anno Domini M^{o} CC^{mo} Nonagesimo primo'). 'Liber monasterii de Ledes (Leeds, Kent) per fratrem Thomam de Meydistane ipsius loci canonicum'.

Engrossing hand (cf. *ECH.*, pl. xix, a) adapted for use in books. Compare with Pl. 1 (i), the less formal variety of the script, and note here the meticulous care with which the hand is written; the emphasis upon calligraphy, (especially in the elaboration of the forked ascenders, and the approach strokes to the head of **f** and long-**s**); and the formation of the minims. The shaft of **t** already protrudes above the headstroke in several instances (1, 'sanat', 7, 'satisfaccionem'), which it does not do in hands of the other variety. This feature was probably borrowed from Textura (cf. Pal. Soc. i, pl. 196, a psalter dated 1284). Characteristic features of this date are: the approach stroke to the right of the forked ascenders, which forms a large loop (**b** in 7, 'Iob'), alongside the occasional hooked ascender (5, 'bone'); **r** with shoulder stroke and descender curving to the left at the foot (13, 'finire'); **d** has a very rounded back and a pronounced diagonal stroke (1, 'domino deo'). Because of the small size of the body of the letters, **a** still extends above the general level of the other letters.

Note the drastic abbreviations in quotations from the text of the Bible (3).

(ll. 1–16) credite in domino deo uestro et securi eritis quia sanat a morbo Marci .5. filia fides tua saluam te fecit et | luce .5. ait dominus paralitico et cetera. vnde dicitur Marci vltimo. signa eos qui crediderunt hec sequentia. in nomine | meo demonia eicient serpentes tollent et si mortiferum quid biberint et cetera.

Dominica eadem. | **Svrge et vade quia fides tua te saluum fecit. luce .xvii^{o}.** In uerbis premissis tria possunt considerari | scilicet bone accionis motus ibi surge. prouectus ibi vade. fructus ibi. fides tua te saluum fecit. ¶ Circa primum nota quod | surgere nos monent a peccato **fetor peccati.** ecclesiastici .xxii^{o}. si coactus fueris in edendo multum. surge scilicet per contricionem | euome scilicet fetorem per confessionem et refrigerabit te scilicet per satisfaccionem. Iob .1. surrexit Iob qui dolens | interpretatur et scidit uestimentum suum scilicet corpus suum per penitencie opera Michee .2. surgite et ite quia hic non | habetis Requiem propterea corrumpetur putredine pessima scilicet populus vnde dicit saluator. Iohannis .xiiii^{o}. | surgite et eamus hinc et psalmo. surgite postquam sederitis ⸢scilicet in luto peccati⸣ qui manducatis panem doloris glosa augustini panem | doloris manducat qui gemit in hac peregrinacione in valle ploracionis ¶ Sunt aliqui porcis consimi|les qui se balniant in peccatorum volutabro de quibus dicitur Ioelis .1. computruerunt Iumenta in stercore suo | putrescere est homines in fetore luxurie vitam finire. psalmo. infixus sum in limo profundi et non est substancia. glosa per ori|ginalia et actualia peccata sunt homines in limis profundi vnde dicitur Petri .2. sus lota in voluta|bro et cetera. ¶ **Timor periculi** geneseos xix[1] surgite egredimini de loco isto quia delebit dominus Ciuitatem hanc | scilicet sodomam peccatricem.

[1] The scribe first wrote 'xxx', and then corrected it by adding a minim over the middle 'x'.

(ii). c. 1315–52. London: British Museum, Royal MS. 14 C xiii, fol. 236^{r}.

Marco Polo, 'De mirabilibus orientalium regionum', in the Latin version of Friar Francesco Pipino of Bologna (*v.* L. F. Benedetto, *Marco Polo, Il Milione* (Florence, 1928), pp. cxxxi ff.). Printed at Cologne, 1671; text of this plate, ibid., p. 27.

Written between *c.* 1315 and 1352. The translation was made *c.* 1315 (*v.* L. F. Benedetto, op. cit.), and the book belonged to Simon Bozoun, Prior of Norwich (fol. 14, 'Liber fratris Symonis Bozoun prioris Norwiciensis'). Since Bozoun ceased to be Prior in 1352, the manuscript must have been written between these dates.

This plate illustrates the transition from the engrossing hand to Anglicana Formata (cf. Pl. 19 (i), dated 1355). Compare with the hand of the previous plate, and note here how the proportions have changed. The body of the letter forms is larger, and the minims are longer and straighter. They are made separately, but the feet are inconspicuous, and sometimes do not appear at all. **a** frequently extends above the general level of the other letters, but the scribe is beginning to realize that with the increase in the size of the hand he can make this complex form within these limits (5, 'Bononia'). Ascenders and descenders are still long compared with later hands, but forked ascenders have been entirely replaced by the hooked form. **r** is much shorter, probably already under the influence of the smaller 'gothic' book hands (Pl. 16 (ii)). **d** has a more upright back than in the previous plate, but it is not yet altogether straight as in Pls. 2 (i); 5 (i).

(ll. 1–15) **Incipit prologus in librum domini Marcipauli de veneciis de condicionibus** | **et consuetudinibus orientalium regionum** |
Librum prudentis honorabilis ac fidelissimi domini Marci Pauli de veneciis de con-|dicionibus orientalium regionum ab eo in uulgari fideliter editum et conscriptum com-|pellor ego frater Franciscus Pipinus de Bononia ordinis fratrum predicatorum a | plerisque patribus et dominis meis ueri⸢di⸣ca et fideli translacione de uulgari ad latinum reducere. vt | qui amplius latino quam uulgari[1] delectantur eloquio. necnon et hii qui propter linguarum veritatem | omnimodam. aut propter diuersitatem et ydiomatum proprietatem lingue alterius intelligere omnino ut | faciliter nequeunt∴ aut delectabilius legant. seu liberius capiant. Porro per seipsos la-|borem hunc quem me assumere compulerunt perficere plenius poterant. Set alciori complecioni va-| cantes et infimis sublimia preferentes∴ sicut terrena sapere. ita terrena describere recusarunt. | Ego autem eorum obtemperans iussioni∴ libri ipsius continenciam fideliter et integraliter ad la-|tinum planum et apertum transtuli∴ quem stilum huius libri materia requirebat. Et ne labor huiusmodi | inanius aut inutilius uideatur∴ consideraui ex libri huius inspeccione fideles viros pos|se multiplicis gracie meritum a domino promereri.

[1] Caret marks above and below **g**.

... [illegible] in Deo vero et [illegible] ... Filia fides tua salvam te fecit. Luce vii. ... Unde [illegible] ... Signa eos qui crediderint hec sequentur. In nomine meo demonia eicient ... et si mortiferum quid biberint ... [illegible] eadem.

Surgens vade quia fides tua te salvum fecit. Luc. xvii. In quibus premissis [illegible] ... bone [illegible] ... Surge, vade, fides tua te salvum fecit. ... [illegible]

Incipit prologus in librum domini Marci Pauli de Veneciis de condicionibus et consuetudinibus orientalium regionum.

Librum prudentis honorabilis ac fidelissimi domini Marci Pauli de Veneciis de condicionibus orientalium regionum ab eo in vulgari fideliter editum et conscriptum compellor ego frater Franciscus Pipinus de Bononia ordinis fratrum predicatorum a plerisque patribus et dominis meis veridica et fideli translatione de vulgari ad latinum reducere, ut qui amplius latino quam vulgari delectantur eloquio, nec non et hii qui propter linguarum varietatem omnimodam aut propter diversitatem ydiomatum proprietate lingue alterius intellectu omnino aut faciliter nequeunt aut delectabilius legant seu libentius capiant. Porro presentes ipsos laborem hunc quem me assumere compulerunt perfecte plenius potuerunt, sed altiori contemplacioni vacantes et infimis sublimia preferentes sicut terrena sapere ita terrena describere recusarunt. Ego autem eorum obtemperans iussioni libri ipsius continenciam fideliter et integraliter ad latinum planum et apertum transtuli, quem stilum huius libri materia requirebat. Et ne labor hic inanis aut inutilis videatur, consideravi ex libri huius inspectione fideles viros posse multiplicis gratie meritum a Domino promereri. Sive quia in varietate decore et magnitudine creaturarum mirabilia Dei aspicientes ipsius poterunt virtutem et sapientiam mirabiliter admirari. Aut videntes gentiles populos tante cecitatis tenebrositate tantisque sordibus involutos gratias Deo agant qui fideles suos luce veritatis illustrans de tam periculosis tenebris vocare dignatus est in admirabile lumen suum. Seu illorum ignorantie condolentes pro illuminatione cordium ipsorum Dominum deprecabuntur. Ut indevotorum quoque christianorum desidia confundetur quia infideles populi promptiores sunt ad venerandum simulacra quam ad ...

5

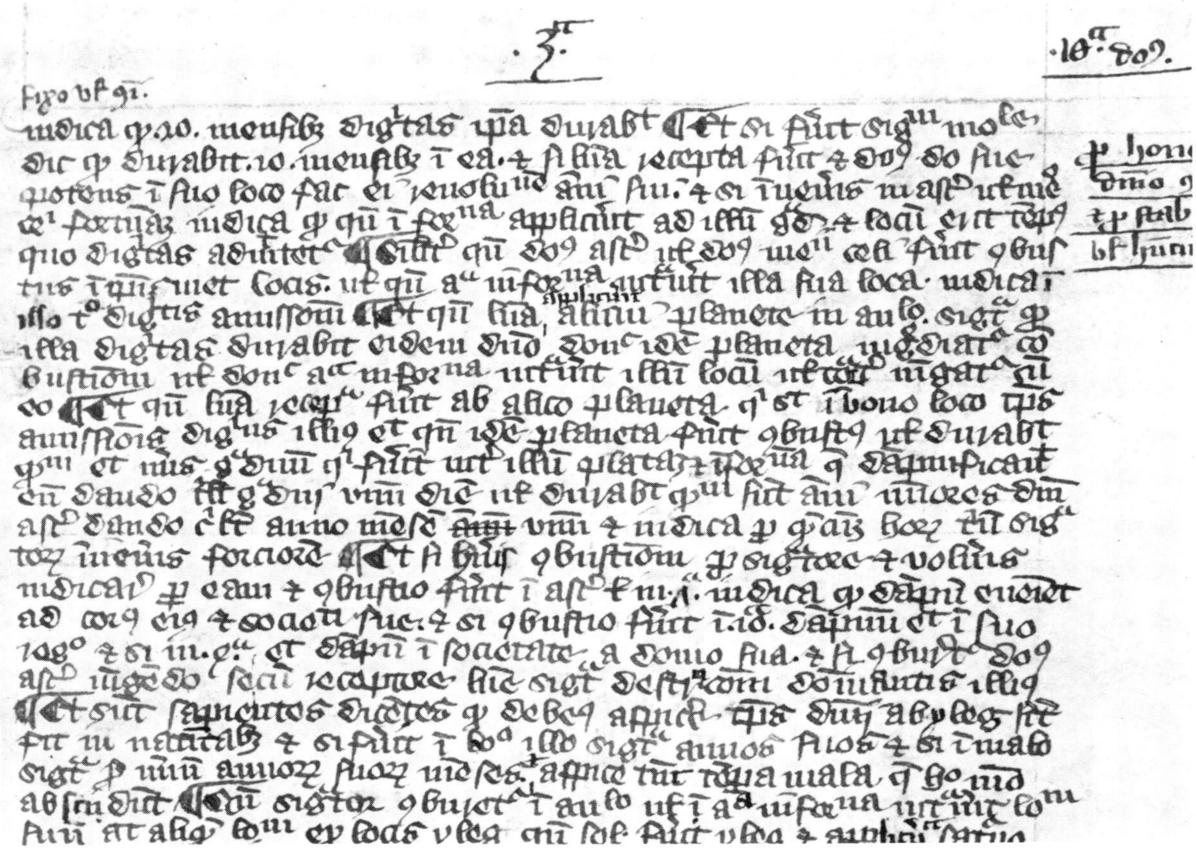

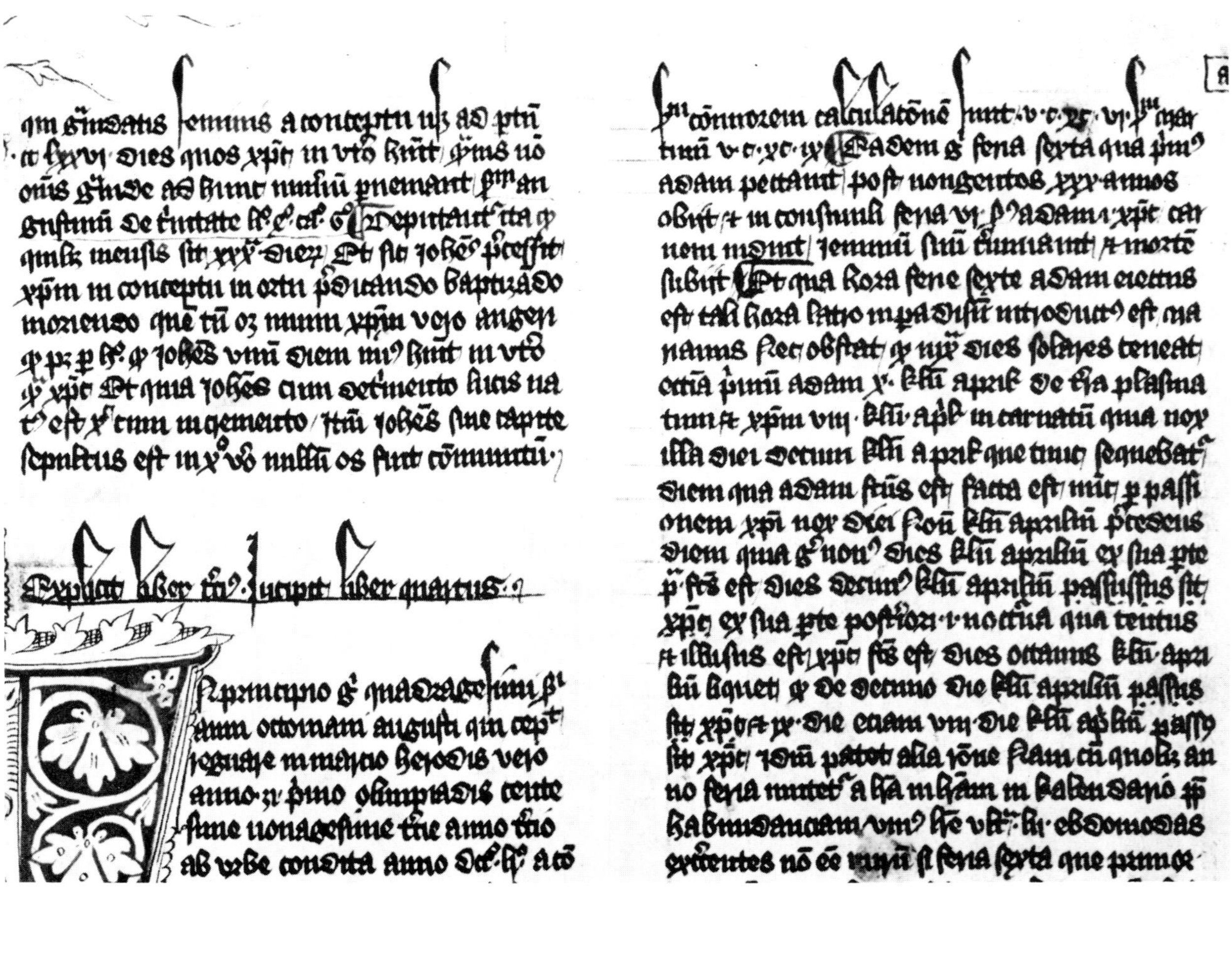

Explicit liber tercius. Incipit liber quartus.

In principio ... anni octouiani augusti ...

5 (i). 1380. Oxford: Corpus Christi College, MS. 151, fol. 62^{r}.

'De iudiciis astrorum', the astrological work of Haly Abenragel translated by Aegidius de Tebaldis and Petrus de Regio from a Spanish version of the original Arabic (Thorndike and Kibre, 475; *v.* Sarton, i (1927), p. 715). Printed at Venice, 1485; text of this plate, ibid., fol. 50^{r}.

Written at Oxford in 1380 (fol. 218^{v}, 'explicit . . . quem librum frater Petrus de Bekklys ordinis beate Marie genitricis Dei de monte Carmeli fecit scribi in civitate Oxoniensi anno Christi m^{o} ccc^{o} octogesimo . . .'. On Beccles, *v.* Emden, *BRUO.*). Subsequently in 1426 the book was given to Peterhouse by John Holbrook (on whom *v.* Emden, *BRUC.*).

Anglicana Formata showing the influence of the smaller 'gothic' book hands (cf. Pl. 16 (ii)). Note the 'squarish' appearance of the letter forms; **a** barely extends above the general level of the other letters; **d** has a straight back (1, 'durabit'); the short form of **s** has been reformed by analogy with the capital form found in the smaller 'gothic' hands (1, 'dignitas'); and the shaft of **t** extends well above the headstroke (2, 'recepta'). The influence of the new style of calligraphy is already noticeable in the broken strokes in the loops of the ascenders, in the lobe of **d** (1, 'durabit'), and the stem of **e** (3, 'potens').

(ll. 1–18) ⌜fixo uel communi⌝ iudica quod .20. mensibus dignitas ipsa durabit ¶ Et si fuerit signum mobile[1] | dic quod durabit .10. mensibus in ea. et si luna recepta fuerit et dominus do(mus) sue | potens in suo loco fac ei reuolucionem anni sui. et si inueneris in ascendente uel medio | celi fortunam iudica quod quando infortuna applicuerit ad illum gradum et locum erit tempus | quo dignitas admittetur ¶ Similiter quando dominus ascendentis uel dominus medii celi fuerit combus|tus in ipsismet locis. uel quando aliqua infortuna intrauerit illa sua loca. iudica in | illo t^{o}[2] dignitatis amissionem ¶ Et quando luna ⌜applicuerit⌝[3] alicui planete in angulo. significat quod | illa dignitas durabit eidem domino donec idem planeta ingrediatur com|bustionem uel donec aliqua infortuna intrauerit illum locum uel corporaliter[4] iungatur cum | eo ¶ Et quando luna recepta[5] fuerit ab alico planeta qui sit in bono[6] loco tempus | amissionis dignitatis illius erit quando idem planeta fuerit combustus uel durabit | quantum erit numerus graduum qui fuerint inter illum planetam et infortunam que dampnificauit | eum dando cuilibet gradus vnum diem uel durabit quantum sunt anni minores domini | ascendentis dando cuilibet anno mensem [annum] vnum et iudica per quemcumque horum trium significa|torum inueneris forciorem. ¶ Et si habueris[7] combustionem pro significatore et uolueris | iudicare per eam et combustio fuerit in ascendente uel in 7^{a}[8] iudica quod damp(n)um eueniet | ad corpus eius et societati sue. et si combustio fuerit in $.10^{a}$. dampnum erit in suo | regno et si in $.4^{a}$. erit dampnum in societate a domo sua.

[1] Headings '$.3^{a}$.' and '$.10^{a}$. domus.'. In margin (only partly visible on plate): 'pro hon(ore uel) | dominio con(sequendo) | et pro stab(ilitate regum) | uel habenci(um dominia) | '.
[2] Printed text has 'illo tempore'. 'in illo' corrected over erasure. Corrector has also added suprascript 'o' after 't' possibly for 'termino'.
[3] Insertion by corrector.
[4] The scribe first wrote the abbreviation for 'totaliter', which has been corrected by inserting 'r' after 'o'.
[5] 'ep' in hand of corrector over erasure.
[6] 'in bo' in hand of corrector over erasure.
[7] 'is' in hand of corrector over erasure.
[8] '7' in hand of corrector.

(ii). c. 1394–97. Oxford: Bodleian Library, MS. Bodley 316 (*SC.* 2752) and London: British Museum, MS. Harley 3634. The plate is from the Bodleian MS., fol. 71^{v}.

Ralph Higden, 'Polychronicon' to 1324 (ed. C. Babington and J. R. Lumby, *Polychronicon Ranulphi Higden*, RS. 41 (London, 1865–6); text of this plate, ibid. iv, pp. 250–4). This text is followed by a Latin Chronicle of England from 1328 to 1388, written in the same hand (ed. E. M. Thompson, *Chronicon Anglie 1328–88 Auctore Monacho Sancti Albani*, RS. 64 (London, 1874).

Written between 1394 and 1397 (*v.* V. H. Galbraith, 'Thomas Walsingham and the S. Albans Chronicle', *English Historical Review*, xlvii (1932), pp. 18–19). On fol. 2 of the Bodley MS., 'Orate pro Thoma duce Gloucestrie qui me dedit huic cantarie siue collegie (*sic*) Sancte Trinitatis infra castrum de Plecy' (i.e. Pleshey, Essex). Thomas of Gloucester died in 1397.

Calligraphic example of Anglicana Formata. The degree of lateral compression is unusual, otherwise most of the features of the hand are characteristic of this date. Ascenders are short, except when decorated (as in the colophon, or on the top line), and are furnished with broken loops. Descenders also are short, especially that of **r** (b, 4, 'feria'). **d** has almost a straight back, and the looped ascender terminates in a short vertical stroke into the lobe of the letter (a, 1, 'ad'). The 'capital' form of short-**s** is made calligraphically (a, 11, 'os'). Note the influence of the new style of calligraphy in the horns on **a** and **c** (a, 1, 'a conceptu'), on **e** (a, 9, 'detrimento'), and occasionally on the heads of **f** and long-**s** (b, 6, 'ferie sexte').

(col. a) qui grauidatis feminis a conceptu usque ad partum | .cc.lxxvi. dies quos Cristus in vtero habuit quamuis non | omnes grauide ad hunc numerum perueniant secundum au|gustinum de trinitate libro 4° capitulo 6° ¶ Deputantur ita quod | quilibet mensis sit $.xxx^{a}$. dierum/ Et sic Iohannes precessit | Cristum in conceptu in ortu predicando baptizando | moriendo quem tamen oportet minui Cristum vero augeri | quod patet per hoc quod Iohannes vnum diem mi(n)us habuit in vtero | quam Cristus Et quia Iohannes cum detrimento lucis na|tus est Cristus cum incremento/ Item Iohannes sine capite | sepultus est in Cristo vero nullum os fuit comminutum. | **Explicit liber tercius. Incipit liber quartus.** In principio igitur quadragesimi secundi | anni octouiani augusti qui cepit | regnare in marcio herodis vero | anno .31. primo olimpiadis cente|sime nonagesime tercie anno tercio | ab vrbe condita anno $dcc^{o}.li^{o}$. a con|

(col. b, ll. 1–14) secundum communiorem calculacionem sunt .v.c.xc.vi. secundum Mart|inum v.c.xc.ix ¶ Eadem igitur feria sexta qua primus | adam peccauit post nongentos xxx. annos | obiit/ et in consimili feria vi. secundus adam id est Cristus car|nem induit/ Ieiunium suum terminauit et mortem | subiit ¶ Et qua hora ferie sexte adam eiectus | est tali hora latro in paradisum introductus est/ Ma|rianus Nec obstat quod iuxta dies solares teneat | ecclesia primum adam x. kalendas aprilis de terra plasma|tum et Cristum viii. kalendas aprilis incarnatum quia nox | illa diei decimi kalendarum aprilium que tunc sequebatur | diem qua adam factus est facta est nunc per passi|onem Cristi nox diei Noni kalendarum aprilium precedens | diem quia ergo nonus dies kalendarum aprilium ex sua parte

6 (i). c. 1445. London: British Museum, MS. Harley 3742, fol. 4^{v}.

Dudo of S. Quentin, 'De moribus et actis primorum Normannie ducum' (ed. *PL.* cxli, 609; text of this plate ibid. 629), to which is added Books v–vii of William of Jumièges, 'De gestis Ducum Normannorum' (*v.* J. Marx, *Guillaume de Jumièges: Gesta Normannorum Ducum*, Société de l'Histoire de Normandie (Rouen, 1914)).

Written at Oxford *c.* 1445 by John Norfolk, Fellow of All Souls College (*v.* Emden *BRUO.*). The scribe has added a treatise of his own at the end of the manuscript, the colophon of which reads (fol. 240^{v}) '. . . sic perfectus est iste tractatus brevissimus in collegio animarum Oxoniensi Anno domini millesimo quadringentesimo quadragesimo quinto quod Norfolk scriptor ac compilator . . .'.

Note the increased influence of Secretary in this hand. Broken strokes occur not only in the lobes of **d** and **q**, but also in **a** (15, 'dacigena'), **c** (14, 'continuis'), **o** (10, 'uoluencium'). Horns occur at points of breaking, especially in **c** (14, 'continuis'), **e** (7, 'exprimatque'), and **q** (6, 'quamuis'). The smaller loops on the ascenders (5, 'calamus'), as opposed to the larger broken loops and hooks, are another feature attributable to Secretary influence. The short **r** derived from the smaller 'gothic' hands (cf. Pl. 16 (ii)) has been remodelled by analogy with the Secretary form.

Dudo wrote a very high-flown Latin style which the scribe (or his predecessor) has not properly understood. Therefore in 6, 'mens' and 16, 'negata' he has substituted more familiar words which resemble graphically those he should be copying, but which do not make sense in the context.

unt Contrita est nanque gens ultore austigno francigena que spurra-|minum (*for* spurcaminum) erat sorde nimium plena Perfidi periurique sunt merito damnati | increduli infideles iuste puniti Prolixum est nobis uniuersorum illius | temporis labores narracione persequi iccirco nostre presumpcionis cicius uer-|tamus stilum ad intencionis propositum Eluciter itaque breuiter calamus | quamuis mens (*for* iners) que nutu dei gesta sunt digeratque compendiose qualiter | acciderunt exprimatque rei ueritatem. spernens sophysmatis errorem | Refutet obscenorum casuum erratus deprimat uenture salutis negocium |
Cum superna deifice trinitatis prouidencia cuius nutu uariata | uoluencium temporum uicissitudine alternantur omnia cerneret | clementer ecclesiam sacro sancto sanguine redemptam sacrique | baptismatis latice profusius emundatam oleique et chrismatis liquore | insigniter delibutam suprascriptis breuiter casibus immaniter afflic-|tam continuis cristianorum precibus suppliciter pulsa non destitit illi sa-|lutifera prebere suffragia ex ferocitatis seue gentilitatis dacigena vt | unde fuerat flebiliter afflicta unde esset uiriliter negata (*for* uegetata) Et quibus | in preceps lapsa his celotenus exaltata Quorum actu flocipensa horum |

(ii). 1475. Glasgow: University Library, Hunterian MS. T. 3. 15 (Young and Aitken, no. 77), fol. 15^{v}.

Nicholas Love, 'The Myrrour of the blessid lif of Ihesu Crist' (Wells, 359 [29]), an English adaptation of the Pseudo-Bonaventura 'Meditaciones Vitae Cristi'. (On Nicholas Love *v.* E. M. Thompson, *The Carthusian Order in England* (London, 1930), p. 339.) The English text ed. L. F. Powell, *Mirrour of the Blessed Lyf of Jesus Christ*, Roxburghe Club (London, 1908), text of this plate, ibid., pp. 23–4.

Written in 1475 by Stephen Doddesham, monk of the Charterhouse of Sheen (fol. iv^{v}, 'thys Boke be longgyth on to the Chartterhows of schene wrettyn be þ^{e} hand of dane stephen doddȝam monke of þ^{e} same plasse the ȝer of Kynge Edward the iiii^{the} xiiii^{the}'). On Doddesham, who also copied Oxford: Trinity College, MS. 46 (a Psalter in a good Textura Quadrata), and Cambridge: University Library, MSS. Dd. 7. 7–10, *v.* Thompson, op. cit., p. 306.

A somewhat idiosyncratic Anglicana Formata hand of the late fifteenth century. Note the exaggeration of the characteristic feet of the minim strokes; the intrusion of Secretary forms, **a** (a, 5, 'Incarnac*io*n'), and short-**s** (a, 4, 'thinges'); and the 'caliper' form of **g** (a, 16, 'gretyng'). Note the changes in the proportions of the body of the letters which have become tall and narrow without being compressed. The pronounced hooks to the ascenders, the long descenders, and the general unevenness of the upright strokes are reminiscent of the hands of the less formal variety of the period (cf. Pl. 3 (ii)).

Note the variations in the spelling of the abbreviated form of the word 'Incarnation', which give to the common mark of abbreviation a different significance (a, 12, 'Incarnac*io*n'; a, 13–14, 'Incar-|nacyou*n*').

(col. a) But thus muche atte thys | tyme sufficith to haue in | mynde. and in contemplac*io*n | of tho thinges that befellen | before the Incarnac*io*n. The | whiche who so wol wel | thenke/ and haue deuoutly | in mynde. and folowe vertu-|ously in dede/ he shal finde | hem ful of gostly fruyt | ¶ Now come we to speke | of the Incarnac*io*n of oure | lorde Ih*es*u. Of the Incar-|nacyou*n* of Ih*es*u / And the feste | of the Anunciac*io*n. And of þe | gretyng Aue maria. Capitulum iii./|

(col. b) instaunce of all' the blessed spi-|rites of heuene. after that | the blessed maiden mary wed-|ded to Ioseph. was goon ho-|me to Nazareth'/ the fader | of heuene called to hym the | Archangel Gabriel. and seide | to him in this man*ere*.¶ Go[1] | to oure der*e* doughter Mary | the spouse of Ioseph'. the | whiche is moost chere to vs | of all' creatures in erthe. and | say to hir that my blessed sone | hath coueited hir shappe. and | hir beute. and chosen hir to | his moder. and therfore p*ra*y |

[1] In margin: 'Petrus | Rauen''.

sunt Contrita est namque gens ultore austrigio francigena que summa-
mum erat sorde nimium plena perfidi pirum que sunt merito dampnati
incredulis infideles iuste puniti Prolixum est nobis immenssorum illi-
temporis labores narracione prosequi immo nisi presumpcionis cicius u-
tamus stilum ad inuencionis propositum Eleuatur itaque breuiter calamus
quamuis meus que nutu dei gesta sunt digeraturque compendiose qualiter
acciderunt exprimaturque rei ueritate. Spernens sophysmatis errorem
Resistet obscenorum casum erratus deprimat nenie salutis negocium
Cum superna deifice trinitatis prudencia cuius nutu narrata
conueniencium temporum uicissitudine alternantur omnia regueret
clementer ecclesiam sacro suo sanguine redemptam sacrique
baptismatis latice perfusius emundatam oleique et chrismatis lignore
insigniter delibutam supra scriptis breuiter casibus nimium afflic-
tam continuis christianorum precibus suppliciter pulsa non destitit illi sa-
lutifera prebere suffragia ex ferocitatis seue gentilitatis dacigena ut
unde fuerat flebiliter afflicta inde esset mirabiliter negata Et quibus
in preceps lapsa hiis celotenus exaltata Quorum actu flecquensa hec

But thus muche atte thys
tyme suffiseth to haue in
mynde. and in contemplacion
of tho thinges that befellen
before the incarnacion. The
whiche who so wol wel
thenke. and haue deuoutly
in mynde. and folowe vertu-
ously in dede. he shal fynde
hem ful of gostly fruyt.
Now come we to speke
of the incarnacion of oure
lorde Jhesu. Of the incar-
nacyon of Jhesu. And the feste
of the Annunciacion. And of pe
gretyng Aue maria. Capitulum iii.

instaunce of all the blessed spi-
rites of heuene. after that
the blessed maiden mary wen-
ded to Joseph. was goon ho-
me to Nazareth. the fader
of heuene called to hym the
Archangel Gabriel. and seide
to hym in this manere. Go
to oure dere doughter mary
the spouse of Joseph. the
whiche is moost chere to vs
of all creatures in erthe. and
say to hir that my blessed sone
hath coueited hir shappe. and
hir beute. and chosen hir to
his moder. and therfore py

Petrus Rauen

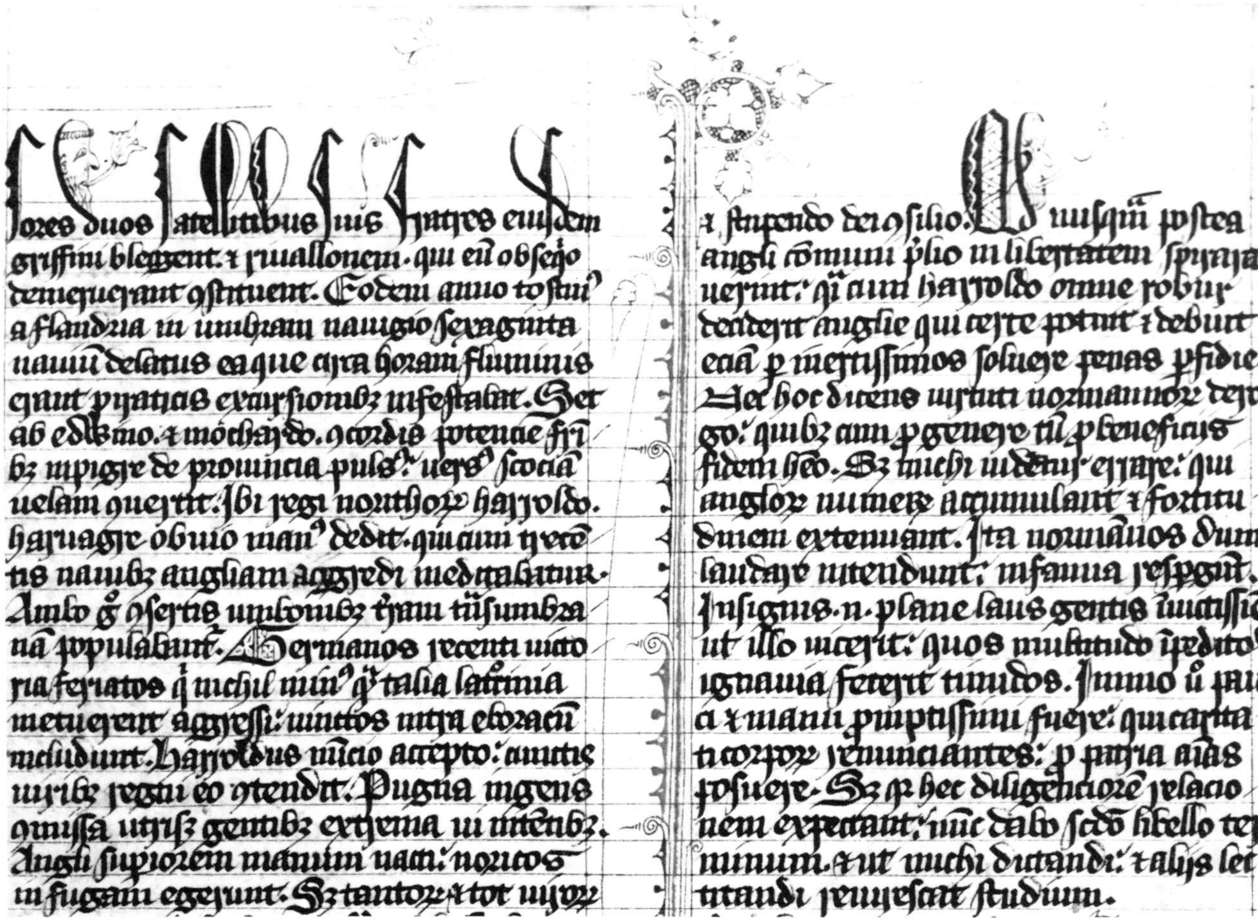

...ores duos satellitibus suis fratres eiusdem griffini blegent et riuallonem. qui eum obsequio demeruerant constituent. Eodem anno tostinus a flandria in humbram nauigio sexaginta nauium delatus ea que circa horam fluminis erant piraticis excursionibus infestabat. Set ab edwino et morkero comitis potentie fratribus impigre de prouincia pulsus: versus scociam velam conuertit. Ibi regi northwegie harroldo haruagre obuio manus dedit. qui cum trecentis nauibus angliam aggredi meditabatur. Ambo ergo consertis unionibus terram transhumbranam populabantur. Germanos recenti victoria feriatos qui nichil minus quam talia latrocinia metuerent aggressi: victos intra eboracum includunt. Harroldus nuncio accepto: cunctis uiribus regni eo contendit. Pugna ingens commissa utrisque gentibus extrema ui nitentibus. Angli superiorem manum nacti: norwegos in fugam egerunt. Set tantorum et tot virorum...

...et stupendo dei consilio. Unius sane postea angli communi prelio in libertatem suspirauerunt: qui cum harroldo omne robur tenderent anglie qui certe potuit et debuit, certa per meritissimos soluere penas perfidie. Nec hoc dicens virtuti normannorum derogo: quibus cum pro genere tum pro beneficiis fidem debeo. Sed michi videntur errare: qui anglorum numerum accumulant et fortitudinem extenuant. Ita normannos dum laudare intendunt: infamia respergunt. Insignis enim plane laus gentis inuictissime ut illos uicerit: quos multitudo impeditos ignauia fecerit timidos. Immo vero pauci et manu promptissimi fuere: qui caritate corporum renunciantes: pro patria animas posuere. Sed quia hec diligentiorem relationem expectant; nunc de secundo libello terminum et ut michi dictandi: et aliis lectitandi renouescat studium.

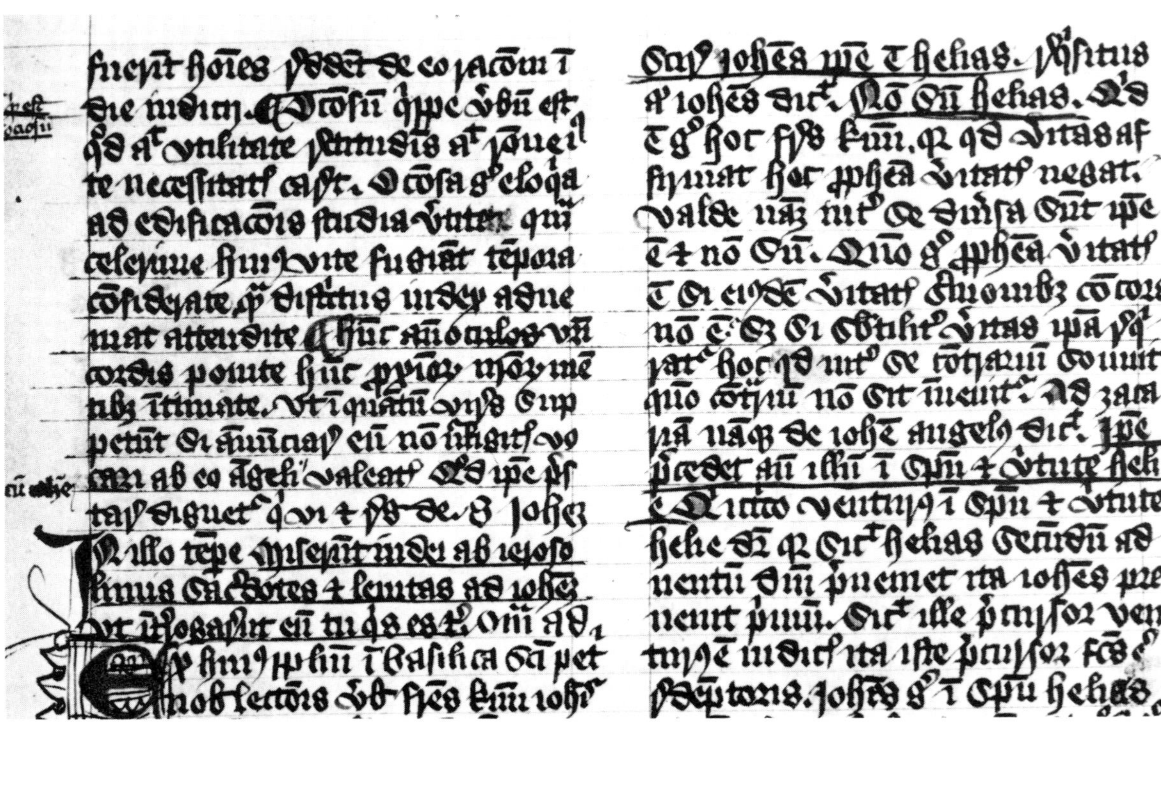

fuerit homines posset de eo iacere in die iudicii. Expositio quippe verbi est ad utilitatem audientis ad iouei te necessitatis capit. Et ... ad edificacionis studia ... qui celestium ... tempora considerate ... districtus iudex adueniat attendite ... cordis ... In ... ab eo ... vero ... Iohannes

In illo tempore miserunt iudei ab ierosolimis sacerdotes et leuitas ad iohannem ut interrogarent eum tu quis es. Omelia ...
Ex huius nobis lectionis verbis fratres karissimi iohannis ...

... iohannes non sum helias. Requisitus a iohannes dicit. Non sum helias. Quis ... et si ... ipse est helias. Quomodo ergo propheta helias non est quem veritas heliam esse perhibet ... Nam zacharias angelus de iohanne dicit. Ipse precedet ante illum in spiritu et virtute helie. ... quia sicut helias secundum aduentum domini preueniet ita iohannes preuenit primum. Sicut ille precursor venturus est iudicis ita iste precursor factus est redemptoris. Iohannes igitur in spiritu helias ...

PLATES 7–8. Bastard Anglicana

7 (i). Mid fourteenth century. Oxford: Bodleian Library, MS. Bodley 712 (*SC.* 2619), fol. 140r.

William of Malmesbury, 'De gestis regum Anglorum' (ed. W. Stubbs, *Willelmi Malmesbiriensis monachi De gestis regum Anglorum*, RS. 90 (London, 1887–9); text of this plate, ibid., i, p. 280).

Written in the mid fourteenth century for Robert Wivill, Bishop of Salisbury 1330–75 (*v.* R. W. Hunt, 'A Manuscript Belonging to Robert Wivill, Bishop of Salisbury', *Bodleian Library Record*, vii (1962), p. 23). The same scribe also copied Oxford: Worcester College, MS. 285 'apud Novam Sarum', but in a different script.

An early attempt to produce Bastard Anglicana, discussed above, p. xviii. Textura features (cf. Pal. Soc. ii, pl. 197; N. Pal. Soc. i, pl. 15) include the verticality of the minims, 'straight-sided' **a** (b, 14, 'ignauia'), bitings (a, 1, 'eiusdem'; b, 1, 'stupendo'), and the use of capital **R** in final positions, particularly at the end of a line (a, 11, 'meditabatuR'; b, 9, 'numeRum'). Anglicana features include **d** with looped ascender, **f**, long-**s**, and **r**. Descenders are long, and turn to the left at the bottom. The features of the two scripts have not been fully assimilated. Note the calligraphic formation of marks of abbreviation and punctuation, and careful attention to details of calligraphy: descenders are extended into hairlines, and otiose hairstrokes appear, especially on final **t** (a, 6, 'erant'). Note also the unusual ligature between **d** and **w** (a, 7, 'edwino').

Contrast the decorative treatment of the ascenders on the top line with those of *c.* 1500 (Pl. 15 (ii)).

(col. a) (succes)sores duos satellitibus suis fratres eiusdem | griffini bleigent. et riuallonem. qui eum obsequio | demeruerant constituent. Eodem anno tostinus | a flandria in umbram nauigio sexaginta | nauium delatus eaque circa horam fluminis | erant piraticis excursionibus infestabat. Set | ab edwino. et mochardo. concordis potencie fratri-|bus inpigre de prouincia pulsus: uersus scociam | uelam conuertit. Ibi regi norithorum harroldo. | haruagre obuio manus dedit. qui cum trecen-|tis nauibus angliam aggredi meditabatuR. | Ambo ergo consertis umbonibus terram transumbra-|nam populabantur. Germanos recenti uicto-|ria feriatos qui nichil minus quam talia latrocinia | metuerent aggressi: uinctos intra eboracum | includunt. Harroldus nuncio accepto: cunctis | uiribus regni eo contendit. Pugna ingens | conmissa utrisque gentibus extrema in intentibus. | Angli superiorem manum nacti: noricos | in fugam egerunt. Set tantorum et tot uirorum |

(col. b) et stupendo dei consilio. Quod nusquam postea | angli communi prelio in libertatem spirara-|uerint (*for* spirauerint): quasi cum harroldo omne robur | deciderit anglie qui certe potuit et debuit | eciam per inertissimos soluere penas perfidie. | Nec hoc dicens uirtuti normannorum dero|go: quibus cum pro genere tum pro beneficiis | fidem habeo. Set michi uidentur errare: qui | anglorum numeRum accumulant et fortitu-|dinem extenuant. Ita normannos dum | laudare intendunt: infamia respergunt. | Insignis enim plane laus gentis inuictissime | ut illo uicerit: quos multitudo impeditos | ignauia fecerit timidos. Immo uero pau|ci et manu promptissimi fuere: qui carita-|ti corporum renunciantes: pro patria animas | posuere. Set quia hec diligenciorem relacio-|nem expectant: nunc dabo secundo libello ter-|minum. et ut michi dictandi: et aliis lec-|titandi reuirescat studium.

(ii). c. 1400. Oxford: Bodleian Library, MS. Bodley 194 (*SC.* 2101), fol. 53r.

Gregory the Great, 'Homiliae xl in Euangelia' (*CPL.* 1711; ed. monachi e congregatione S. Mauri, *S. Gregorii Magni Opera Omnia*, nova recensio quam procuravit J. B. Gallicciolli (Venice, 1768–76), tom. v; text of this plate, ibid., pp. 164–6, also *PL.* lxxvi, 1098–9).

Written *c.* 1400 (for similar examples of this style in documents *v. ECH.*, pl. xxx, a, dated 1381; and N. Pal. Soc. i, pl. 225, dated 1394. In the documents the descenders are much longer than those in the book.).

Fully developed Bastard Anglicana hand discussed above, p xviii. Compare with the previous plate and note here how the details of the two scripts have been completely assimilated. Note especially the treatment of the minim strokes, the calligraphy in the formation of marks of abbreviation and punctuation, and the cursive habit of using short **s** at the beginning of a word. Note also the influence of the new style of calligraphy in the occasional presence of broken strokes in the lobes of **a** (b, 3, 'veritas') and **d** (a, 3, 'rectitudinis'), and in the horn which appears occasionally on the top of **e** (b, 7, 'eiusdem').

(col. a) fuerint homines reddent de eo racionem in | die iudicii. ¶ Ociosum[1] quippe verbum est | quod aut vtilitate rectitudinis aut racione ius|te necessitatis caret. Ociosa ergo eloquia | ad edificacionis studia vertite[te] quam | celerime huius vite fugiant tempora | considerate. quam districtus iudex adue|niat attendite ¶ hunc ante oculos vestri | cordis ponite hunc proximorum nostrorum men|tibus intimate. Vt in quantum vires sup|petunt si annunciare eum non necligitis vo|cari ab eo angeli ⌜cum iohanne⌝[2] valeatis Quod ipse pres|tare dignetur qui vivit et regnat deus.

Secundum Iohannem | In illo tempore **Miserunt iudei ab ieroso|limis sacerdotes et leuitas ad iohannem | vt interrogarent eum tu quis es et cetera. Omelia ad | populum in basilica sancti petri** | EX huius | nobis lectionis verbis fratres karissimi iohannis |

(col. b, ll. 1–16) **scire Iohannes ipse est helias.** requisitus | autem iohannes dicit. **Non sum helias.** Quid | est ergo hoc fratres karissimi. quia quod veritas af-|firmat hoc propheta veritatis negat. | valde namque inter se diuersa sunt ipse | est et non sum. Quomodo ergo propheta veritatis | est si eiusdem veritatis sermonibus concors | non est? set si subtiliter veritas ipsa requi-| ratur hoc quod inter se contrarium sonuit | quomodo contrarium non sit inuenitur. Ad zaca-|riam namque de iohanne angelus dicit. **Ipse** | **precedet ante illum in spiritu et virtute heli|e** Qui iccirco venturus in spiritu et virtute | helie dicitur quia sicut helias secundum ad-|uentum domini preueniet ita iohannes pre-|uenit primum.

[1] In margin (only partly visible on plate), '(Nota) quid est | (verbum) ociosum.'

[2] Inserted in the margin with signe de renvoi in the text.

8 (i). Second half of the fifteenth century. Oxford: Bodleian Library, MS. Rawlinson C. 398, fol. 49r.

The Latin 'Brut', here called 'Nova Chronica de Gestis Regum Anglorum' (*v.* C. L. Kingsford, *English Historical Literature in the Fifteenth Century* (Oxford, 1913), pp. 310 ff., who also prints the text of this plate, ibid., p. 315).

Written probably early in the second half of the fifteenth century (the chronicle ends in 1434, *v.* Kingsford, op. cit.). The book formerly belonged to Sir John Fortescue (*v. Fortescue on The Governance of England*, ed. C. Plummer (Oxford, 1885), p. 180).

Note the difference between this hand and Anglicana Formata (Pl. 6 (i)), especially the greater emphasis here on calligraphic features (cf. treatment of descenders), and the characteristic 'Bastard' treatment of the minim (17, 'Normanniam', cf. previous plate), although it is not carried out consistently. The hand has been strongly influenced by the new calligraphy, and especially Bastard Secretary. Note the short **r** form, the replacement of the broken stroke in the lobe of **d** by a calligraphic curve (2, 'die'), the treatment of the stem of **a**, and the lobes of the letter formed by means of elaborate broken strokes (1, 'victoriam'), the horns on **a**, **e**, and **t** (5, 'Wallie,' 'et'), and the short **s** formed by means of broken strokes (5, 'Comes'). The absence of the looped ascender to **d** is characteristic of the second half of the century (cf. Pls. 12 (ii); 14 (i); and 15 (ii) and (ii)).

contra dictum Ducem Aurelianensem victoriam obtinuerunt ¶ Anno | quartodecimo Rex iste infirmitate insanabili arreptus vicesimo die Maii | apud Westmonasterium spiritum exalauit et in ecclesia Cristi Cantuarie honorifice | tumulatur
HEnricus quintus filius Henrici iiiiti Princeps | Wallie Dux Cornubie et Comes Cestrie apud Monemouth in | Wallia natus vicesimo die Marcii videlicet in festo sancti Cuthberti Episcopi et | Confessoris accidente tamen Dominica in passione domini apud Westmonasterium | coronatur. ¶ Anno primo huius Regis insurrexerunt plurimi lollardi | ipsum Regem et Clerum sui Regni occidere et destruere proponentes sed diui-|no mediante auxilio infra breue penitus sunt extincti. ¶ Anno tercio | huius Regis Comes Cantebrigie frater Ducis Eboracensis Dominus le Scroop | Thesaurarius Anglie et Thomas Grey Miles ipsum Regem francigenis | pro vno Millione auri vendiderunt ac ipsum et fratres suos interficere subi-|to proposuerunt. Qui propterea capti et morti adiudicati apud Suthhampto-|niam capitibus sunt truncati. Quo facto mox Rex ille cum multitudine naui-|um ad numerum Mille et quingentarum et potestate magna versus Hareflieu in | Normanniam nauigauit et apud Kitcaws applicuit. ac villam de Hareflieu | obsedit diris insultibus ipsam infestando Cuius parietes horribilibus bumbar-|(dorum)

(ii). c. 1500. Oxford: Bodleian Library, MS. Laud Misc. 517, fol. 126v.

'The Manere of Good Lyuynge', a translation of the Pseudo-Bernard 'Tractatus de modo bene vivendi' (*v. PL.* clxxxiv, 1199).

Written *c.* 1500 by William Darker. The hand is the same as that of Brit. Mus. Additional MS. 22121 which is signed by Darker. He entered the Carthusian order and became a monk of Sheen (*v.* E. M. Thompson, *The Carthusian Order in England* (London, 1930), p. 333). Other manuscripts copied by Darker include: Cambridge: Pembroke College, MS. 221, University Library, MS. Ff. 6. 33; Glasgow: University Library, Hunterian MS. T. 6. 18; Brit. Mus., Cotton MS. Caligula A ii, fols. 204r–6v; Lambeth Palace Library, MS. 546, fols. 57r–77v; Bodl. MS. Laud Misc. 38.

Fere-textura, an example of the kind of idiosyncratic handwriting produced at this period, which replaced Bastard Anglicana as a calligraphic substitute for Textura. The handwriting is a skilful amalgam of elements from various kinds of handwriting. The form of **d** in 1, 'loued', and the treatment of occasional minims and mainstrokes (e.g. the second **i** in 5, 'signifyed', and the **l** in 7, 'ladder') are from Bastard Anglicana. **g** (2, 'god'), **f** and long-**s**, **h** with hooked ascender (3, 'The'), and the form of **r** (6, 'differre') are from Anglicana Formata. The form of **d** in 7, 'ladder', horned **e** (1, 'loued'), and final short-**s** (2, 'ys') are from Secretary. The proportions of the hand are those of the cursive scripts, but the over-riding impression is that of Textura, an impression which stems from the accent on vertical strokes, and such details as the form of **a**, and the simple straight ascenders.

For an earlier example of Fere-textura, equally idiosyncratic, *v.* Wright, *EVH.*, pl. 19.

Note the otiose strokes in this late hand, especially the hairline through final **h** (1, 'mouth'), and the firm stroke added to final **g** (7, 'stondyng').

from yo*ur* mouth'.// My loued sust*ere* in cryste | god ys yo*ur* laude. so þt alwey hys lawde and | pr*a*yesyng' be in your' mouth'. Amen. **The | liii exhortac*io*n ys of actyfe ⁊ conte*m*platyue | lyves. signifyed by Iacob ladder and shew-|yth howe they doo differre.** | Iacob sawe a ladder stondyng' vpon þe grou*n*de | and aungelle of god goyng' vp ⁊ down' *per*by. | and the toppe of hit to hys semyng' tow-|chyd the fyrmament.// In this ladder be all' | thoo putte: that be ordeyned to com' to heuen. |and eu*ery* p*er*sone that loketh' after heuen: hath' | a place in this ladder. Thys ladder ys the | vniu*er*sall' chyrch' of cryste. which' in parte |

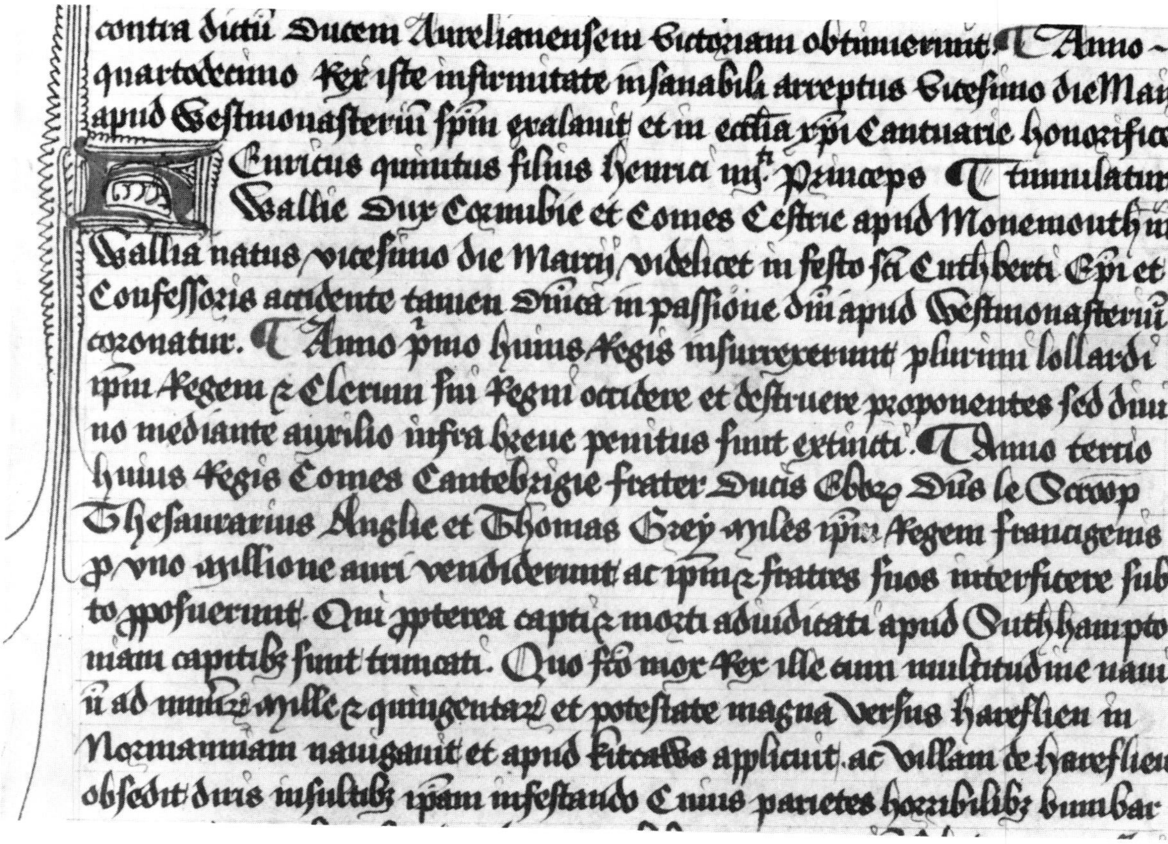

contra dictum Ducem Aurelianensem victoriam obtinuerunt. ¶ Anno
quartodecimo Rex iste infirmitate insanabili arreptus vicesimo die Maii
apud Westmonasterium spiritum exalavit et in ecclesia Christi Cantuarie honorifice
Henricus quintus filius Henrici iiij Princeps ¶ tumulatur
Wallie Dux Cornubie et Comes Cestrie apud Monemouth in
Wallia natus, vicesimo die Marcii, videlicet in festo sancti Cuthberti Episcopi et
Confessoris accidente tamen Dominica in passione domini apud Westmonasterium
coronatur. ¶ Anno primo huius Regis insurrexerunt plurimi lollardi
ipsum Regem et Clerum sui Regni occidere et destruere proponentes sed divi
no mediante auxilio infra breue penitus sunt extincti. ¶ Anno tercio
huius Regis Comes Cantebrigie frater Ducis Ebor' Dominus le Scroop
Thesaurarius Anglie et Thomas Grey miles ipsum Regem francigenis
pro uno millione auri vendiderunt ac ipsum et fratres suos interficere subi
to proposuerunt. Qui propterea capti et morti adiudicati apud Suthhampto
nam capitibus sunt truncati. Quo facto mox Rex ille cum multitudine navi
um ad numerum mille et quingentarum et potestate magna versus Hareflieu in
Normanniam navigavit et apud Kitcaws applicuit ac villam de Hareflieu
obsedit diris insultibus ipsam infestando Cuius parietes horribilibus bumbar

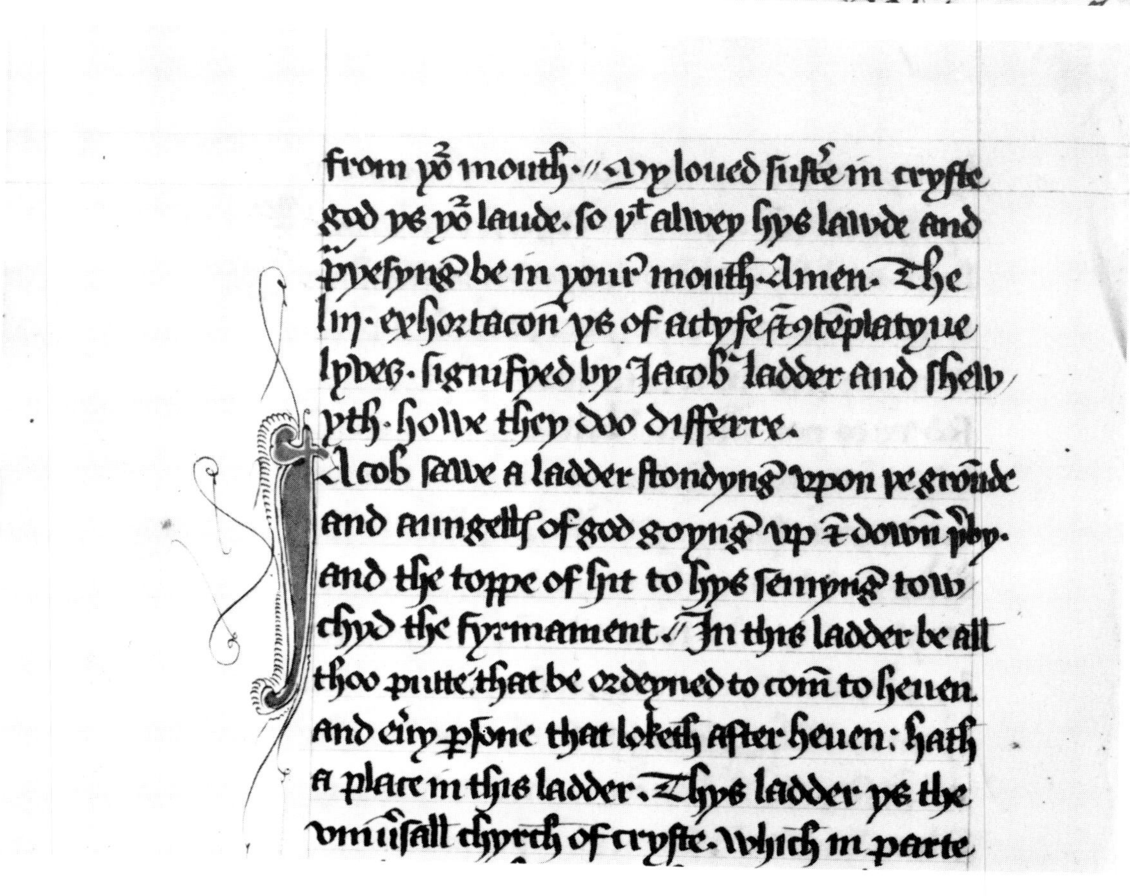

from your mouth. // My loued suster in cryste
god ys your laude. so that alwey hys lawde and
praysyng be in your mouth. Amen. The
iij. exhortacon ys of actyfe and contemplatyve
lyves. signifyed by Jacob ladder and shew
yth howe they doo differre.
Jacob sawe a ladder stondyng vpon the grounde
and aungells of god goyng vp and down therby.
and the toppe of hit to hys semyng tow
chyd the fyrmament. // In this ladder be all
thoo persones that be ordeyned to com to heuen.
And euery persone that loketh after heuen: hath
a place in this ladder. Thys ladder ys the
vniuersall chyrch of cryste. which in parte

Bona est oracio cum ieiunio et elemosina unde et hiis duabus alis secundum Augustinum volat ad divinam maiestatem. Verum in oracione votum mentis magis quam sonus oris in ieiunio mortificacio viciorum magis quam abstinencia ciborum et in elemosina affectus magis quam census a sancte devocionis cultoribus attenditur, vos ergo fratres carissimi [illegible] in virtute sancte obediencie committimus et mandamus firmiter iniungentes, quatinus omnibus et singulis confratribus vestris et coepiscopis nostris et ecclesie nostre Cantuariensis suffraganeis, cum omni celeritate qua poteritis, visis presentibus harum seriem communicantes mandetis ut ipsorum singuli in ecclesiis suis cathedralibus et aliis suarum civitatum et diocesium, suos subditos quoscumque clericos tam religiosos quam seculares et eciam laicos efficaciter moneant et induci moneri faciant et inducant, ut ipsi pacem [illegible] regni Anglie in missis solempnibus sermonibus et processionibus publicis singulis quartis et sextis feriis ea de causa faciendis specialiter et devote recommendatam habeant, Deum quod omnipotentem ac matrem suam gloriosam virginem Mariam omnesque sanctos et sanctas dei corde puro et mente devota in eorum oracionibus pro pace eadem celerius et feliciter optinenda, ac pro salubri statu domini domini nostri Regis, et bona ac prospera regni sui gubernacione, et ecclesie Anglicane nec

Thomas permissione divina Cantuariensis Archiepiscopus tocius &c. Dilectis in Christo filiis magistris Ricardo Brynkele [illegible] generali, Willelmo Bocombe advocato curie nostre Cantuariensis, et Roberto Wytton [illegible] salutem &c. Ad cognoscendum et procedendum in quadam causa appellacionis [illegible] non admissionis dilecti filii domini Johannis [illegible] capellani [illegible] ad ecclesiam parochialem de [illegible] Lincolniensis diocesis ut dicitur vacantem per illustrissimum in Christo principem dominum Henricum dei gratia Regem Anglie et Francie et dominum Hibernie illustrem, verum ipsius ecclesie hac vice ut pretenditur patronum et in possessione iuris seu quasi presentandi ad eandem bona fide existentem venerabili fratri nostro domino Henrico dei gratia Lincolniensi episcopo loci diocesano rite et legitime ut asseritur presentati et non admissi ad nos et nostram audienciam interiecte, iuxta formam appellacionis [illegible] partibus [illegible] ac principalem causam [illegible] et negocium principale eiusdem cum omnibus suis incidentibus emergentibus dependentibus et connexis audiendum discuciendum et fine debito terminandum, necnon ad inquirendum seu inquiri faciendum in forma iuris de et super vacacione dicte ecclesie ac aliis articulis in hac parte necessariis et consuetis, vocatis in hac parte de iure vocandis, et si per eandem inquisicionem aut

PLATES 9–10. The Development of Secretary as Determined by Hands in Documents

9 (i). 1375–81. London: Lambeth Palace Library, Register of Archbishop Sudbury, fol. 42^{r}.

Mandate to the Bishop of London to pray for the King (printed in Wilkins's *Concilia*, iii, p. 121).

The influence of French developments in cursive handwriting is apparent first in features of style rather than letter forms. The body of the letter forms is narrow and short in relation to the ascenders and descenders. There is a general impression of rigidity, which is due partly to the fine connecting strokes between the letters and partly to the scribe's lack of familiarity with the new script. The rigidity and lateral compression are less noticeable in books than in documents (cf. Pl. 11 (i)). In the early stages of Secretary in this country the better-known graphs belonging to the Anglicana script (particularly **r**, **g**, and **w**) survive for a time in place of the less well known but more characteristic graphs of the new script (5, 'suffraganeis', 'celeritate'). Note the early form of **a** in which the first movement of the lobe stroke descends at a steep angle (1, 'Bona'). Ascenders are furnished with pronounced hooks, proper to Anglicana, and descenders are long and narrow. The shaft of the letter **t** is upright and rarely protrudes above the headstroke (5, 'Cantuariensis').

(ii). 1396–1414. London: Lambeth Palace Library, Register of Archbishop Arundel, fol. 135^{r}.

Commission to Richard Brinkley, Examiner General of the Court of Canterbury, and others to inquire into the reasons why John Newlyn had not been admitted to the vacant living of Dorney, Berks.

Towards the end of the fourteenth century a number of hands show considerable sophistication. The desired effect is achieved first and foremost by greater punctiliousness in writing the script. Attention was paid to the angle at which the pen was held, to the beginning and conclusion of each stroke, and to the symmetry of adjacent strokes. Letter forms were elaborated, becoming more complex as breaking was introduced into strokes other than those forming the lobes of letters, as in the stems of **a**, **g**, and **r** (1, 'Cantuariensis', 'Magistris', 4, 'illustrissimum'). The treatment of minims should be noted, and especially those in final positions (4, 'Lincolniensis'). The **g** with diamond shaped lobe (4, 'gratia'), and the form of **r** with broken stem are characteristic of this date.

10 (i). 1414–43. London: Lambeth Palace Library, Register of Archbishop Chichele, fol. 17ʳ.

Profession of Obedience to the See of Canterbury made by Bendict Nicholl on his translation to the diocese of S. Davids (1417).

Cf. Pls. 11 (ii); 19 (ii).

The most prominent feature of the hands at this period is the conspicuous attention to superficial details of style. Horns were formed wherever possible on the tops (**e** in 1, 'vero') and even lobes of letters (**d**, in 2, 'pandam'), thus giving the hands a characteristic prickly appearance. There are also certain important changes in the structure of the letter forms. The horned **g** (3, 'Legatum') now predominates over the form with diamond shaped lobe, and the tail of the letter curves to the right. The shaft of **t** is now curved and extends above the headstroke (2, 'petri'). The 'v'-shaped form of **r** now becomes the most common form of the letter in English hands (1, 'vero'), predominating over the form with broken stem.

(ii). 1443–54. London: Lambeth Palace Library, Register of Archbishops Stafford and Kemp, fol. 20ʳ.

Profession of Obedience to the See of Canterbury made by Adam Moleyns on his election to the bishopric of Chichester in 1446.

Cf. Pls. 12 (i); 20 (i); 22 (i).

The hands of the middle of the century are small, and the body of the letter forms is better proportioned and less compressed than in the earlier periods, but the splay of the hands is more exaggerated. The letter forms are much simpler than in earlier or later hands. Horns are usually omitted. Ascenders are short, curved, and furnished with a small loop. The descenders are wide, often short, and taper and slope are exaggerated. Note **d** with simple ascender.

(iii). 1454–86. London: Lambeth Palace Library, Register of Archbishop Bourgchier, fol. 118ʳ.

The institution of John Mesaunt as Rector of High Hardes (Upper Hardres) Kent in 1478.

Cf. Pls. 12 (ii); 13 (i) and (ii).

The proportions of the hands have again altered. The body of the letter forms is short and wide, giving hands of this time the characteristic appearance of having been squashed from above. Ascenders and descenders are once again long in relation to the body of the letters. The hands become even more current. Cursive forms are used wherever possible (**e**, in 1, 'mensis'). Despite this currency superficial details of style were once again emphasized. Horns reappear on the letter forms, and were frequently exaggerated. Note the forms of **d** and **t** (5, 'dicit'), and the approach strokes to initial **i**, **m**, and **n** (6, 'in').

capcione. Consilium vero quod michi credituri sunt per se vel nuncios seu litteras ad eorum dampnum
me sciente nemini pandam. Papatum romanum et regalia sancti petri adiutor eis ero ad retinendum et defendendum salvo meo ordine contra omnem hominem. Legatum apostolice sedis in eundo et rede-
undo honorifice tractabo et in suis necessitatibus adiuvabo. Vocatus ad synodum veniam nisi prepedi-
tus fuero canonica prepedicione. Apostolorum limina romana curia existente citra singulis annis ul-
tra vero montes singulis bienniis visitabo aut per me aut per meum nuncium nisi apostolica absolvar
licencia. Possessiones vero ad mensam mei episcopatus pertinentes non vendam neque donabo neque in-
pignorabo neque de novo infeudabo vel aliquo modo alienabo inconsulto Romano pontifice. Sic

In dei nomine Amen. Ego Adam Moleyns ecclesie Cicestrensis electus et a vobis Reverendissimo patre Johanne dei
gracia Cantuariensi archiepiscopo tocius Anglie primate et apostolice sedis Legato eiusdem ecclesie Cicestrensis consecrandus antistes
vobis et successoribus vestris archiepiscopis Cantuariensibus in ipsa ecclesia canonice instituendis et sancte Cantuariensis ecclesie metro-
politice debitam et canonicam obedienciam reverenciam et subieccionem me per omnia exhibiturum profiteor et
promitto secundum decreta Romanorum pontificum vestrique Cantuariensis archiepiscopi ac successorum vestrorum et predicte
sancte Cantuariensis ecclesie iurium adiutor ero ad defendendum retinendum et conservandum Salvo ordine meo Sic me
deus adiuvet et hec sancta dei euangelia Et hec omnia subscribendo manu propria confirmo

Item xxvij(no) die mensis Marcii Anno domini millesimo CCCC lxxvij(no) apud Knoll admissus
fuit magister Johannes Aresamt presbiter in decretis bacallarius ad ecclesiam prebendalem de Hith-
harder Cantuariensis diocesis per mortem magistri Ricardi Drayton ultimi Rectoris eiusdem vacantem et ad
presentacionem precelse nobilisque domine domine Anne ducisse Bukinghm comitisse Hereford
Stafford et Northampton ut dicitur spectantem Ipsumque admissum instituit et fecit Rectorem canonice
in eadem cum suis Iuribus et pertinenciis universis Curamque et regimen animarum parochianorum etc. Et
recepto ab eodem canonice obediencie iuramento Scriptum fuit Archidiacono Cantuariensi seu eius officiali etc.

natoris lib. xi. c. fortassis inducie primi sunt etiam indigentem sibi esse ab eo petendo molestum scriptura dicente Etiam proximo suo pauper odiosus erit prov. xiiii c. quanto magis nollet sic molestari ab aliquo non egente set indigenciam confingente cum spontanee mendicaret. Item iniuriam videntur eos inferre vere et non sponte mendicis quia ea que eis debentur in sue necessitatis articulo ipsi ad voluptatem exposcunt atque mendicando recipiunt. Item ut michi videtur tenentur tales mendicantes spontanee statim egentibus erogare omne quod eis superfluum preter preceptum Quod superest date elemosinam et sicut supra in secundo articulo primus ac ut michi videtur probabile ipsi constituentis in iudicio a sinistris dicetur Esurivi et non dedisti michi manducare Mt. xxv c. Et hoc quasi paupere bonum habere in talibus qui mendicant spontanee et habent edificia tamquam regum palacia piscinas ampliores comitibus ecclesias sumptuosiores cathedralibus ornamenta plura ac nobiliora civitatis mundi platis duo viri fortassis exceptis libros plures et meliores quibuscumque platis atque magis campanilia sumptuositatis immense claustra valde sumptuosa duplicia in quorum deambulatoriis equites armati cum lanceis erectis possunt libere placitare preciosiorem vestitum quasi civitatis.

ter. merito ergo repellitur quia maledicto dignus est qui ... et impedit opus quod negligenter pertractant exequendo. Considerandum ergo utrum bonitas sit repellenda ab opere negligente an eo retinendo et ymaginem vere ... ex aliis summam artibus. Sciat medicus egroti quod negligencia et desidia medici ius alti vulneris serpit. Quanto ergo melius removere huiusmodi medicum qui tepidus tepit cum presertim nulla conveniat consolatio ut cuiquam officium ad eum medicum transferat qui maturius possit egroto sua diligencia subvenire. Nomine clemencior est qui repellit nichil proficientem quam qui retinet ad discrimen egroti. Constituit aliquis prepositum edificantibus operariis et tepentibus qui debeat suum opus explicare. Utrum ne tunc probabilior videtur si diligentem instituat. Ideo si forte maiori subintererit de hiis qui operantur in domo aliqua construenda repellat eum melius cordens ne edificare quam perhabentibus primus edificatum dissolvat atque aliquem in eius substituat locum qui cum diligencia edificet. Similiter et tertium prepositum propulsore negligencium et substituat diligentes ne longa tertium corrumpat mensura ne magis probabis quam illum qui desides in sua negligencia perseverare paciatur. Transi nunc ad eos qui mandata edificent et legem intelligunt et animam ... receperint salvanda. Nomine est primus eorum edificet domum Dei cum iusticia teneat indumentum cum diligencia sanc

PLATES 11–13. Secretary Book Hands

11 (i). c. 1400. Oxford: Bodleian Library, MS. Bodley 144 (*SC.* 1914), fol. 117[r].

Richard Fitzralph, Armachanus, 'Sermones' (*v.* A. Gwynn, 'The Sermon Diary of Richard Fitzralph', *Proceedings of the Royal Irish Academy*, xliv, sect. C, Dublin (1937), p. 2). On Fitzralph, *v.* Emden, *BRUO.*

Written *c.* 1400. The manuscript formerly belonged to Simon Maidstone, monk of S. Augustine's, Canterbury. (Dom Simon Maidstone was ordained deacon, March 1445, priest, September 1447. He was sacristan of S. Augustine's in 1458, granger 1459–60, and almoner 1468–9. *v.* Register of Archbishop J. Stafford, Cant. fols. 198[v], 201[v]; and C. Cotton, 'S. Austin's Abbey, Canterbury, Treasurers' Accounts 1468–9', *Archaeologia Cantiana*, li (1940), pp. 78, 86, 90, 104.)

Early book hand of the Secretary script. The hand is much more fluent than those of the documents (cf. Pl. 9 (i) and (ii)), highly current, but well spaced and regular. Note the comparative absence of splay, and of Anglicana graphs of **a**, **g**, **r**, and short-**s**. Letter forms characteristic of Secretary hands of this date include **g** with diamond-shaped lobe, here resolved by currency (1, 'indigentem'), the form of **r** with broken stem (4, 'iniuriam'), and the form of **t** in which the shaft barely protrudes above the headstroke (14, 'cathedralibus'). The ascenders, curved forward at the top and furnished with pronounced hooks, and the long, narrow descenders are characteristic of both Anglicana and Secretary hands of this period. Despite the fact that some of the features of the script have been affected by currency, such as the letter **a** which has lost its broken lobe (6, 'ad'), note the calligraphic treatment of final minims (4, '-digenciam', 'cum'), and of the descender of the letter **h** (7, 'michi').'

uatoris luce xi aut fortassis meridie proximum suum eciam indigentem sibi esse ab | eo petendo molestum scriptura dicente **Eciam proximo suo pauper odiosus erit** | prouerbiorum xiiii capitulo quanto magis nollet sic molestari ab aliquo non egente set in-|digenciam confingente cum spontanee mendicaret Item iniuriam videntur | tales inferre vere scilicet non sponte mendicis [..] cum ea que eis debentur in sue | necessitatis articulo ipsi ad voluptatem exposcunt atque mendicando recipiunt | Item vt michi videtur tenentur taliter mendicata spontanee statim egen|tibus erogare cum sint eis superflua propter preceptum **Quod superest date** | **elemosinam** et cetera sicut supra in secundo articulo. ymmo aliter vt michi | videtur probabile ipsis constitutis in iudicio a sinistris dicetur **Esuriui et** | **non dedisti michi manducare** et cetera Matthei xxv. capitulo et hoc suasi precipue lo-|cum habere in talibus qui mendicant spontanee et habea(nt)[1] edificia tan|quam regum palacia pistrinas ampliores comitibus ecclesias sumptuosiores | cathedralibus ornamenta plura ac nobiliora cunctis mundi prelatis | domino nostra papa fortassis excepto libros plures et meliores quibuscumque | prelatis atque magistris campanilia sumptuositatis inmense claustra | valde sumptuosa duplicia in quorum deambulatoriis equites armati cum | lanceis erectis possunt libere preliari preciosiorum vestitum quasi cunctis |

[1] The scribe has omitted the n and written c for t.

(ii). Second quarter of the fifteenth century. Cambridge: Gonville and Caius College, MS. 99/51, p. 11.

Ambrose, 'In Psalmum CXVIII Expositio' (*CPL.* 141; ed. M. Petschenig, *CSEL.* lxii; text of this plate, ibid., p. 32, also *PL.* xv, 1217).

Written in England in the second quarter of the fifteenth century (cf. Pl. 10 (i)). A *terminus ante quem* is provided by the fact that Walter Crome added fols. 311–97 to this book in his own hand in 1446 (on Crome, *v.* Emden, *BRUC.*).

Typical Secretary book hand of the period. Note the emphasis on superficial details of style, especially the horns at the tops of the letters **e** (3, 'retineri') and **t** (1, 'impedit'), and the horned **g** form (2–3, 'negli-|gentem') which had replaced the form with diamond-shaped lobe in most hands by this period. Note also the appearance of the Anglicana graphs of **a** (8, 'aliquem'), **g**, and **r** (8, 'egroti').

ter. Merito ergo repellitur quia maledicto dignus est quia polluit magis et impedit opus quod | negligenter putauerit exequendum. Consideremus ergo vtrum bonitas sit repelli ab opere negli-|gentem an vero retineri et ymaginem rei huius ex aliis sumamus artibus. Curat medicus | egrotum set negligenter et desideria medici ius alti vulneris serpit. Quanto igitur melius | remoueri huiusmodi medicum qui tempus terit cum perfectum nullum senciat vulneratus. | vt curandi officium ad eum medicum transferatur. qui maturius possit egroto sua diligencia | subuenire. Nonne clemencior est qui repellit nichil proficientem. quam qui retinet ad dis|crimen egroti Constitue aliquem prepositum edificantibus vel eciam texentibus qui debeat summam | operis explicare. Vtrum is tibi probabilior videtur si diligenter insistat. Acsi quam forte incu|riosum aduerterit de hiis que operantur in domo aliqua construenda. repellat eum melius | cordens non edificare quam rihantibus (*for* hiantibus) rimis edificata dissolui atque aliquem in eis sub-|stituat locum qui cum diligencia edificet. Similiter eciam trextrini (*for* textrini) prepositum prepulsorem (*for* repulsorem) negli|gencium vt substituat diligentes ne longa textr(i)-num corrumpat incuria non magis | probabis quam illum qui desides in sua negligencia perseuerare paciatur. Transi nunc ad | eos qui mandata edificant et legem intexunt et animam vniuscuiusque receperunt saluandam | Nonne si quis eorum edificet domum dei cum iusticia texat indumentum cum diligencia sanet |

12 (i). **Mid fifteenth century.** Oxford: Bodleian Library, MS. Rawlinson Poetry 149 (*SC.* 14641), fol. 97[r].

Geoffrey Chaucer, 'The Canterbury Tales' (*v.* W. McCormick and J. Heseltine, *The Manuscripts of Chaucer's Canterbury Tales* (Oxford, 1933), p. 433; J. Manly and E. Rickert, *The Text of the Canterbury Tales* (Chicago, 1940), i, p. 455). Text of this plate from 'Pardoner's Tale', *CT.* C, lines 692–720.

Written in the mid fifteenth century (cf. Pl. 10 (ii)) by William Stevens (fol. 136[v] 'Expliciunt fabula scripta per Willm Stevenns.' The name is in mirror writing.).

Typical example of the small, simple hands of the mid fifteenth century. Note the exaggeration of the splay, and of the taper and slope of the descenders of **f**, **p**, and **s**; the ascenders furnished with small loops; the omission of horns; and the simplified letter forms of headless **a** (3, 'shal'), tailless **g** (24, 'god'), and **w** (15, 'towarde'). **d**, however, retains its looped ascender (14, 'drynkyn').

Note the inconsistency in the scribe's use of 'capital' letters, especially at the beginning of the lines.

ye goddes armes quod this riatour'
Is it soche peril with hym forto mete
I shal hym seche be sty and be strete
I make a vow be the digne goddes bones
herkenith felawes we thre be al ones
late iche of vs holde vp his honde til othir
And ich of vs become othres brothir
And we wil slee this fals traitore deth
he shal be slayn he that so many sleeth
Be godes dignite or it be night
togidre haue thise thre her trouthe plight
to leve and to die ilke of hem with othir
As thogh he were his oune borne brothir
And vp thei sterten and drynkyn in this rage
And forthe thei gone towarde that village
Of which the taverner' hath spoke before
And many a griseli othe than haue thei swore
And cristes blissed bodi thei torent
that dede shal be dethe if thei may hym hent
when thei haue gone not fulli a myle
Right as thei wolde haue troden ouer' a stile
An olde and a pore man with hem met
this olde man ful mekeli hem gret
And saide thus now lordes god yow see
the proudest of thise riatours thre
Answered ayen what cherle with hardi grace
whi arte thou al forwrapped save thi face
whi levest thou so longe in so grete age
this olde man gan loke in his visage

(ii). **c. 1470.** Oxford: Bodleian Library, MS. Rawlinson Poetry 32 (*SC.* 14526), fol. 65[v].

'The Brut' in English down to the accession of Edward IV in 1461 (Wells, 206 [10]; ed. F. W. D. Brie, *The Brut or the Chronicles of England*, E.E.T.S. (o.s.), 131, 136; text of this plate, ibid. 131, p. 18, l. 28).

Written *c.* 1470 (cf. Pl. 10 (iii)).

Note the combination of fluency and style in this well-written hand. The letter forms have the characteristic appearance of having been squashed from above. Note the disappearance of hairlines in the construction of letters, especially the letter **e** (2, 'euer'). Note also the simplified ascender of the letter **d** (5, 'and'), the tall shaft of **t** extending well above the headstroke (2, 'that'), the heavy ascender of **v** (10, 'vnto'), and the way in which the loops of the ascenders tend to lean forwards (4, 'his'). Despite the fluency of the hand there are many calligraphic features: bitings (1, 'made'), otiose strokes over medial **h** (which are not represented in the transcription) (3, 'dought*er*'), as well as on final letters; a calligraphic version of short **r** which looks forward to the sixteenth-century form (7, 'her') (cf. Pl. 20 (ii)); and pronounced approach strokes to initial letters (12, 'man').

Again note the inconsistency in the use of 'capital' letters (3, 'Dwelled', but 8, 'leyer').

The word 'good' in the last line provides a good example of the problem afforded by the tendency to add strokes to final letters for calligraphic effect, as well as to signify an abbreviation (*v.* p. xxix). The stroke added to the final **d** could signify the plural ending (-es, -is, -ys), but the singular *good* was used with the meaning 'property', 'wealth', at this time (*v.* examples quoted in *OED.*, sb. Good, C. 7, b, c, d, and 8 spec.).

And thanne he made sorow and Dole ynow w[t] sore We-|pyng' and saide allas that euer I came into this lande for yet | I had leuer to haue Dwelled' stille with my eldest dought*er:* | And thanne Rigan his Doughter herd that and she came to | him in grete angur' and swore by god' and by his holidome and' | by alle that she myght swere. that he shulde haue no moo | but o knyght if he wulde abide with her'. Thanne beganne | kyng' leyer' sore to wepe ageyne and made mech Dole *7* sorow | and saide allas now haue I leued' to long' that this sorow mys-|chef' and shame is thus befalle vnto me' now. For now I am | pover' that sumtyme was riche and al men honowred' me *7* | worshipped' me whanne I was reche And no man now set no | price by me but hath me in skorne and in Derision wherefor' | now haue I nether frende ne no kynne that will do any thing' | for me but haue me in skorne and in despite And now I know | wele that Cordeille my yongest dought*er* saide to me trawth' | whanne she said that her Susters flatered' w[t] me And also | whanne she said' as meche as I was worthy to be loued' so | meche shulde I be beloued' of her'. For alle the while that I | had good' I was wel-beloued' and worshipped' for my reches |

Ye goddes armes quod this riatoure
Is it soche peril with hym forto mete
I shal hym seche be sty and be strete
I make avow be the digne goddes bones
Herkenith felawes we thre be al ones
Late iche of vs holde vp his honde til other
And ich of vs become others brother
And we wil slee this fals traytore deth
He shal be slayn he that so many sleeth
Be goddes dignite or it be nyght
Togidre haue these thre her trouthe plight
To leve and to die ilke of hem with other
As thogh he were his owne borne brother
And vp thei sterten and dronkyn in this rage
And forthe thei gone towarde that village
Of which the taverner hath spoke before
And many a grisely othe than haue thei swore
And cristes blissed body thei to rent
That dede shal be dethe if thei may hym hent
When thei haue gone not fulli a myle
Right as thei wolde haue troden over a stile
An olde and a pore man with hem met
This olde man ful mekeli hem gret
And saide thus now lordes god yow see
The proudest of these riatours thre
Answered ayen what cherle with harde grace
Whi arte thou al for wrapped save thi face
Whi levest thou so longe in so grete age
This olde man gan loke in his visage

And thanne he made sorow and dole ynow wt the kyng and said allas that euer I came in to this land for yet I had leuer to haue dwelled stille with my eldest doughter. And thanne Regan his doughter herd that and she came to him in grete angre and swore by god and by hir holidome and by alle that she myght swere that he shulde haue no moo but o knyght if he wolde abide with her. Thanne bigann kyng leyer sore to wepe ageyne and made mich dole & sorow and said allas now haue I lived to long that this sorow & mischif and shame is thus befalle vn to me now. ffor now am I pover that sumtyme was riche and al men honowred me & worshipped me whanne I was riche and no man now set no pris by me but hath me in skorne and in derision wherfor now haue I nether frende ne no kynne that will do any thing for me but haue me in skorne and in despite and now I knowe wele that Cordalle my yongest doughter said to me trawth whanne she said that her sustres flatered wt me and also whanne she said as miche as I was worthy to be loued so miche shulde I be beloued of her. ffor alle the while that I had good I was wel beloued and worshipped for my richis

13

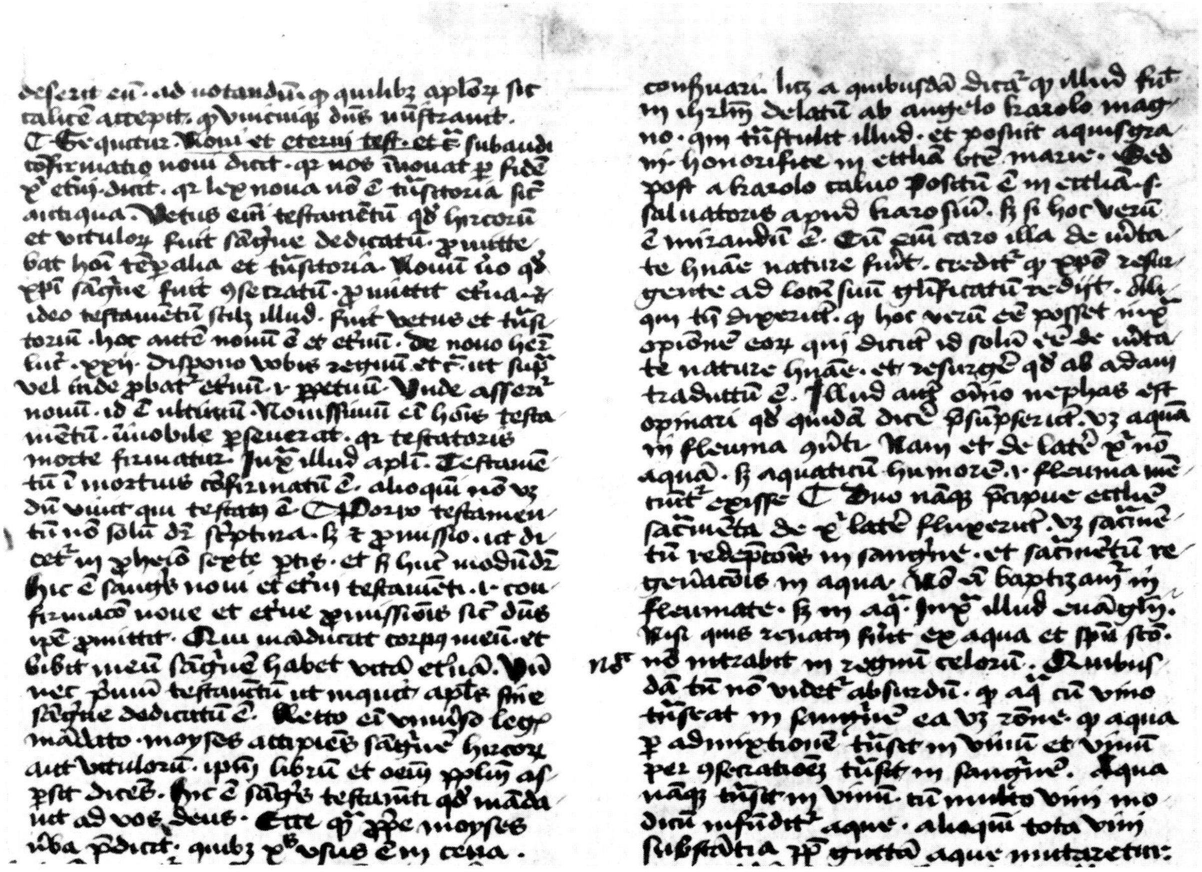

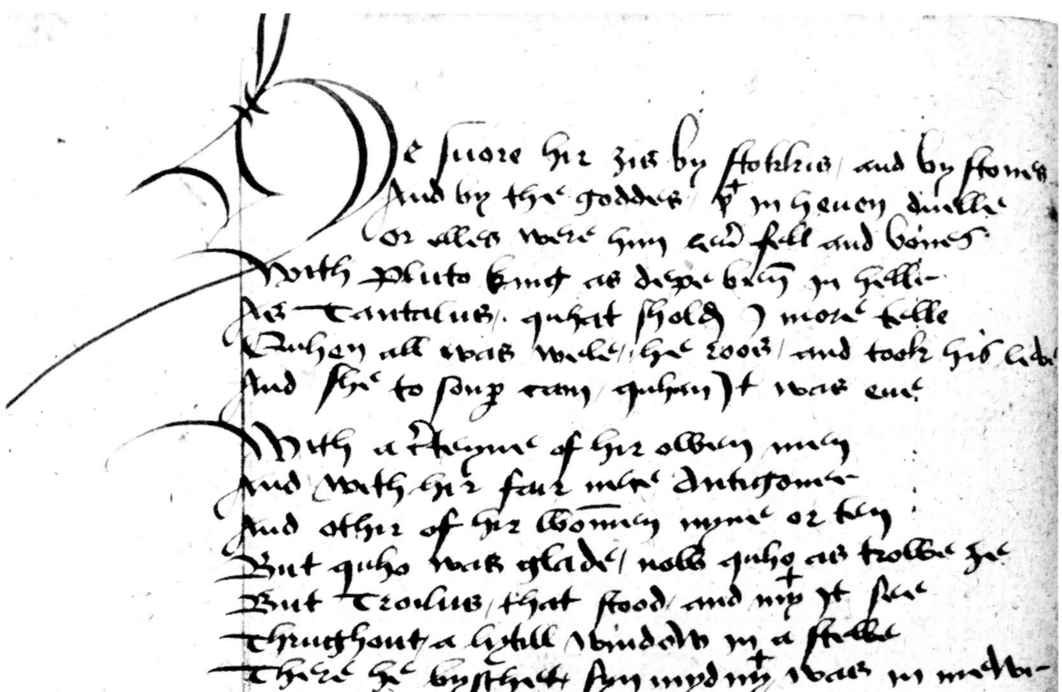

13 (i). 1470. Oxford: Bodleian Library, MS. Laud Misc. 100, fol. 76r.

Gulielmus Durandus, 'Rationale Divinorum Officiorum' (printed at Venice, 1485; text of this plate, ibid., sig. i, 6).

Written in 1470 by Robert de Kyngorn (fol. 199v, 'Explicit presens rationalis diuinorum codex officiorum per Robertum de Kyngorn' capellanum [auctoritate apostolica notarium publicum] Anno Domini Millesimo quadringentesimo sep'tu'agesimo ac eciam mensis uero nouembris die duodecimo et cetera').

A smaller and more current hand than that of the previous plate, but showing similar general characteristics. The body of the letter forms is short and wide, and the ascenders and descenders are long in relation to it. Despite the currency there is a suggestion of horns at the 'corners' of the letters.

The most striking feature of the hand is the presence of simple upright ascenders which have not been furnished with loops or hooks. This feature is found in numerous manuscripts written in Secretary from 1470 onwards (cf. Pl. 15 (ii)). Other dated hands containing this feature include Oxford: Magdalen Coll., MS. Lat. 49 (1471); Lincoln Coll., MS. Lat. 102 (1482); and Bodl., MS. Bodley 831 (1493). Although such ascenders are characteristic of the humanist script, the presence of such forms at this date in hands other than those of known humanists, or in hands which do not also have humanist capital forms, does not necessarily indicate humanist influence.

(col. a, ll. 1–26) deserit eum. ad notandium quod quilibet apostolorum sic | calicem accepit. quod vnicuique dominus ministrauit. | ¶ Sequitur. **Noui et eterni testamenti. et cetera** subaudi | confirmatio noui dicit. quia nos innouat per fidem | Cristi eterni. dicit. quia lex noua non est transitoria sicut | antiqua. Vetus enim testamentum quod hircorum | et vitulorum fuit sanguine dedicatum. promitte-|bat homini temporalia et transitoria. Nouum uero quod | Cristi sanguine fuit consecratum. promittit eterna. et | ideo testamentum scilicet illud. fuit vetus et transi-|torium. hoc autem nouum est et eternum. De nouo habetur | luce .xxii. Dispono vobis regnum et cetera ut supra | vel inde probatur eternum id est perpetuum. Vnde asseritur | nouum. id est ultimum. Nouissimum enim hominis testa-|mentum. immobile perseuerat. quia testatoris | morte firmatur. Iuxta illud apostoli. Testamen-|tum in mortuis confirmatum est. alioquin non valet | dum viuit qui testatus est. ¶ Porro testamen-|tum non solum dicitur scriptura. sed et promissio. ut di-|cetur in prohemio sexte partis. et secundum hunc modum dicitur | Hic est sanguis noui et eterni testamenti id est con-|firmacio noue et eterne promissionis sicut dominus | ipse promittit. Qui manducat corpus meum. et | bibit meum sanguinem habet vitam eternam. Vnde | nec primum testamentum ut inquit apostolus sine | sanguine dedicatum est.

(col. b, ll. 1–27) conseruari. licet a quibusdam dicatur quod illud fuit | in iherusalem delatum ab angelo karolo mag-|no. qui transtulit illud. et posuit aquisgra-|ni honorifice in ecclesia beate marie. Sed | post a karolo caluo Positum est in ecclesia sancti | saluatoris apud karosium. sed si hoc verum | est mirandum est. Cum enim caro illa de uerita-|te humane nature fuerit. creditur quod Cristo resur-|gente ad locum suum glorificatum rediit. Ali-|qui tamen dixerunt. quod hoc verum esse posset iuxta | opinionem eorum qui dicunt id solum esse de verita-|te nature humane. et resurgere quod ab adam | traductum est. Illud autem omnino nephas est | opinari quod quidam dicere presumpserunt. videlicet aquam | in fleuma conuerti Nam et de latere Cristi non | aquam. sed aquaticum humorem id est fleuma men-|ciuntur exisse ¶ Duo namque precipue ecclesie | sacramenta de Cristi latere fluxerunt. videlicet sacramen-|tum redempcionis in sanguine. et sacramentum re-|generacionis in aqua. Non enim baptizamur in | fleumate. sed in aqua. Iuxta illud euangeli. | Nisi quis renatus fuerit ex aqua et spiritu sancto. | non[1] intrabit in regnum celorum. Quibus-|dam tamen non videtur absurdum. quod aqua cum vino | transeat in sanguinem ea videlicet racione. quod aqua | per admixtionem transit in vinum et vinum | per consecrationem transit in sanguinem.

[1] 'Nota' in central margin.

(ii). c. 1488. Oxford: Bodleian Library, MS. Arch. Selden B. 24 (*SC.* 3354), fol. 49v.

Geoffrey Chaucer, 'Troilus and Criseyde', and other poems. Known as the 'Sinclair Manuscript', since the arms of the Scots family of Sinclair appear on fol. 118v, and the names of various of its members on fols. 79, 230v, and 231r,v (*v.* Hammond (1908), pp. 341–3. The manuscript has been described, with facsimile, by R. K. Root, *The MSS. of Chaucer's Troilus* (1914), p. 43.). Text of this plate from 'Troilus and Criseyde', Book III, lines 589–602.

Written in Scotland by the scribe who also copied the 'Haye' manuscript (see Ker, *Medieval MSS. in British Libraries*, ii, 1), shortly after 1488 (fol. 120r 'Natiuitatis principis nostri Iacobi quarti anno domini M^mo iiii^c lxxii^o xvii die mensis marcii videlicet in festo sancti patricii confessoris in monasterio sancte crucis prope Edinburgh'. James IV came to the throne in 1488.).

A typical Scottish hand of the end of the fifteenth century betraying, much more than contemporary English hands, the influence of developments which had taken place in French document hands during the course of the fifteenth century (*v.* p. xxi). Note the form of **c**, consisting of two short strokes placed at right angles with a short diagonal stroke placed on the 'back' of the letter (8, '*cer*teyne'), and the further exaggeration of the horns at the tops of letters, especially **e** (cf. 3, 'were' with Pl. 12 (ii), 2, 'euer') and **t** (cf. 5, 'telle' with Pl. 12 (ii), 2, 'that'). When the hand is written currently, as here, the letter **e** tends to come apart: the stem of the letter becomes attached to the preceding letter, and the headstroke to the following letter (3, 'leu*er*'; 9, 'nece'; 14, 'There'). These French features passed into the 'Tudor' Secretary in the sixteenth century. Note that initial **i** always descends below the line; the two forms of **w** (9, 'with', 10, 'wo*m*men'); and the distinction between **sc** and **st** in ligature (13, 'stewe', 14, 'byschet').

He suore hir ʒis by stokkis/ and by stones
And by the goddes/ þt in heuen duelle
Or elles were him leu*er* fell and bones
With Pluto king as depe ben' in helle
As Tantalus/. quhat shold' I more telle
Quhen all was wele/. he roos/ and took his leve
And she to soup*er* cam/ quhan It was eue.

With a *cer*teyne of hir owen men
And with hir fair nece Antigonee
And othir of hir wo*m*men nyne or ten
But quho was glade/ now quho as trowe ʒe
But Troilus/ that stood/ and my*ght* it see
Thrughout a lytill window in a stewe
There he byschet syn mydny*ght* was in mewe

PLATES 14–15. Bastard Secretary

14 (i). c. 1415. Oxford: Bodleian Library, MS. Bodley 596 (*SC.* 2376), fol. 2^{r}.

'The Lyf of Adam' (Wells, 320 [66]. Printed from this manuscript, *Archiv* lxxiv, p. 345; text of this plate, ibid., p. 346. Ed. from Brit. Mus. Additional MS. 39574 by M. Day, *The Wheatley MS.*, E.E.T.S. (O.S.), 155, p. 76, who discusses this text, p. xxii; text of this plate, ibid., p. 81.).

Written *c.* 1415. The manuscript contains various historical pieces (*v.* C. L. Kingsford, *English Historical Literature in the Fifteenth Century* (Oxford, 1913), p. 87), including lists of the Mayors, Bailiffs, and Sheriffs of the City of London (fols. 53^{v}–65^{v}). The last entry of the lists which is written in the handwriting illustrated in this plate is for the year 1415 (fol. 61^{v}). On fol. 1^{r} are the arms of the Baron family (on whom *v.* A. I. Doyle, 'Books Connected with the Vere Family and Barking Abbey', *Essex Archaeological Society's Transactions*, xxv (1958), p. 228).

An early attempt to produce a Bastard form of Secretary, betraying considerable influence of Bastard Anglicana (cf. Pl. 7 (ii)). Note the appearance of Anglicana forms of **a**, **g**, **r**, and **s** alongside those of Secretary (6, 'Adam', 14, 'myght', 7, 'fro', 6, 'sle'). The treatment of the minims still closely resembles that found in Bastard Anglicana. Other Bastard Anglicana features include the letter **d** (4, 'seide Adam'), and the uprightness of the descenders of **f** and long-**s**. Note the close attention to details of calligraphy: the sophisticated manner in which the descenders of **g** and **h** have been prolonged into hairlines; the carefully formed horns at points of breaking (in **a**, 16, 'and', and the shaft of **t**, 17, 'noght to'); the sophisticated form of cursive **e** (1, 'Thanne'); the presence of otiose hairlines such as those descending from '2'-shaped **r** (1, 'lord'), those forming the approach stroke to **m** (6, 'my'), and those after final letters (after 1, 'efte').

Other examples of this kind of handwriting may be seen in G. C. Macaulay, *The English Works of John Gower*, i, E.E.T.S. (E.S.), 81, frontispiece; and in Pal. Soc. ii, pl. 57.

¶ Thanne seid Eue to Adam efte. my lord I dye for | hungre. wolde god I myght dye or elles p^{t} I were | slayn of the forwhy for me is god wroth w^{t} the. | ¶ And thanne seide Adam: grete is in heuen and in | erthe his wrethe. Wher' it be for me or for the I note | ¶ And 'Then'[1] seide Eue to Adam. my lord sle me p^{t} I may | be done away fro the face of god and fro the sight | of his aungeles. so that he may forgete to be wro-|the with the oure lord god ȝete so that happely he | lede the in paradys. for why: for the cause of me *pou* | art putte oute therof. Thanne seide Adam 'To'[1] Eue | speke no more so. lest oure lord god sende his malisou*n* | vppon vs / How myght it be that I myght myne | hoonde in my fleshe. pat is to sayne: how myght | it be p^{t} I shuld slee myne owen flesshe. But arise | go we and seche wher' w^{t} for to lyue and ne stynt | we noght to seche They went and soght. but pei | fonde noght. als thei hadde in paradys. Neuerthelees |

[1] Inserted in the margin with signe de renvoi in the text.

(ii). Mid fifteenth century. Oxford: Bodleian Library, MS. Hatton 2 (*SC.* 4130), fol. 24^{v}, col. b.

The treatise of Boccaccio, 'De Casibus Virorum Illustrium', rendered into English verse by John Lydgate and called 'The Fall of Princes' (*v.* H. Bergen, *Lydgate's Fall of Princes*, part iv, E.E.T.S. (E.S.), 124, p. 73, where the manuscript is listed under the obsolete reference no. MS. Hatton 105). Text of this plate from Book I, lines 4075–88.

Written in the mid fifteenth century. The stylistic features of this hand are closely similar to those of a hand used for the heading of an entry dated 1453 which occurs on fol. 225^{r} of the Register of Archbishop Kemp, preserved in Lambeth Palace Library.

An example of the version of Bastard Secretary, which was developed by English scribes (*v.* p. xxi). There are no traces in this hand of parallel developments which were taking place on the Continent. This hand is composed of enlarged forms of the less formal variety of the script with the features of Textura Quadrata (cf. Pl. 22 (ii)) superimposed upon them. The influence of Textura can be seen in the emphasis upon vertical strokes (especially in the distortion of the letter **a**, 11, 'as'); the proportions of the body of the letters; and the treatment of minims (1, 'writing') and of the feet of mainstrokes (as in **w** in 4, 'waile'). Note the attention to details of calligraphy: the hairlines added to final letters, and to the descending limb of **h**; and the idiosyncratic treatment of the tail of **g**. Note that although these otiose strokes are traced as hairlines, the stroke through **ll** (5, 'all', and 8 'full') is traced firmly.

¶ And in thy writing leue me nat behinde
Nor in thy boke that thou nat disdeine
Among tho folk that thou haue me in my*n*de
Which that for sorwe wepe waile ⁊ pleine
And thus Thiestes rehersing all' his peine
Liche as he wold him self on peces rende
Made vnto Bochas of his tale an ende

¶ Atreus after with a full' pale chere
And of enuie full' ded in his visage
Vnto Iohn' Bochas he gan approch nere
Liche as he had befallen in a rage
And furiously abraid in his language
Hou may this be that like a man were wode
Thiestes hath his venym sowe abrode

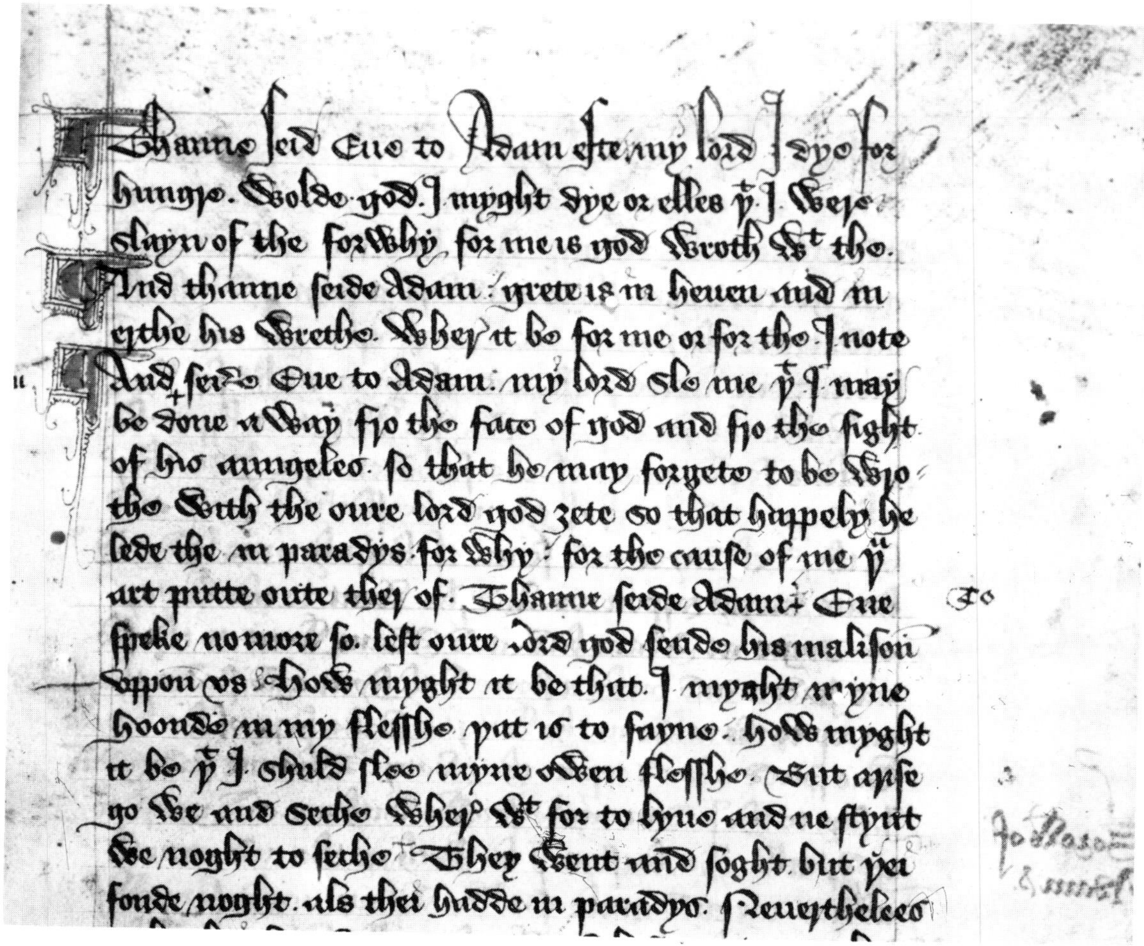

Thanne seid Eue to Adam efte, my lord I dye for
hungre. Wolde god I myght dye or elles þt I were
slayn of the. forwhy, for me is god wroth wt the.
And thanne seide Adam: grete is in heuen and in
erthe his wrethe. wher it be for me or for the I note.
And seide Eue to Adam: my lord sle me þt I may
be done away fro the face of god and fro the sight
of his angeles. so that he may forgete to be wro
the with the oure lord god zete so that happely he
lede the in paradys. forwhy: for the cause of me þu
art putte oute ther of. Thanne seide Adam: Eue
speke no more so. lest oure lord god sende his malison
uppon us. how myght it be that I myght wryne
hoonde in my flesshe pat is to sayne. how myght
it be þt I shuld slee myne owen flesshe. But arise
go we and seche wher wt for to lyue and ne stynt
we noght to seche. They went and soght. but þei
founde noght. als thei hadde in paradys. Neuertheles

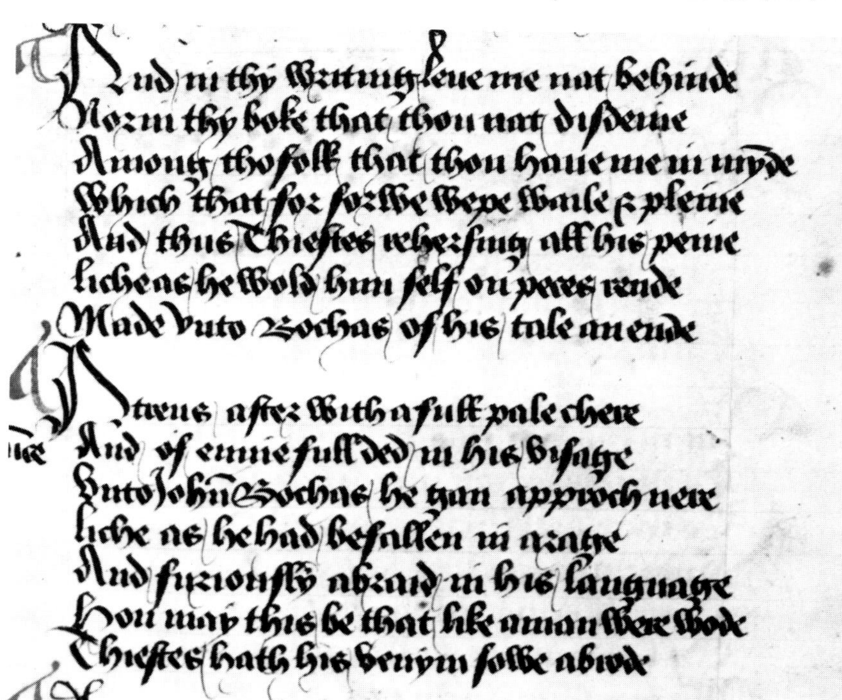

And in thy writyng leue me nat behynde
Nor in thy boke that thou nat disseure
Among tho folk that thou haue me in mynde
Which that for forthe were waile & pleine
And thus Thiestes whersing all his peine
Liche as he wold him self on peces rende
Made unto Bochas of his tale an ende

Atreus after with a full pale chere
And of enuie full ded in his visage
Unto John Bochas he gan approch nere
Liche as he had befallen in a rage
And furiously abraid in his language
How may this be that like a man were wode
Thiestes hath his venym so abrode

15

Demonesque maxime in cibo et potu hominibus insidiantur. et eos decipiunt. effugiabis. Aut enim multos per immoderatam assumptionem alimentorum a vigore virtutis deiciunt. aut per nimiam abstinentiam in ipsa virtute franguntur. Multi enim sunt qui in eadem re fluctuant. ut aut nimis aut magis sumant continue et formam vivendi nunquam retinent. Sed nunc hoc. nunc illud melius putant. Estimant enim insipientes et indocti qui dulcedinem amoris Christi nunquam experti sunt. quod

Haue gouernaunce of all worldly ryches.
Agayne folke unkynde loke that ye dysdayne.
Suffre them not haue non interesse.
For to approch to youre hygh noblenes.
For there ys no vyce more hatefull to conclude.
Than is the vyce of ingratitude.

Consulo quisquis eris qui pacis federa queris.
Consimilis esto lupis cum quibus esse cupis.

Counsayll what so euyr thou be.
Of polycye foresyght and prudence.
If thou wylt lyue in peace and vnyte.
Conforme thy selfe and thynke on this sentence.
Where so euer thou holde resydence.
Amonge wolles be wolwysshe of courage.
Lyon with lyons a lambe for Innocence.
Lyke the audyence so utter thy language.

The unycorne is caught with the maydens songe.

15 (i). **Mid fifteenth century.** Oxford: Bodleian Library, MS. Bodley 456 (*SC.* 2412), fol. 9^{r}.

Richard Rolle, 'Emendatio Vitae' (*v.* Allen (1927), p. 232; Printed at the end of *Speculum Spiritualium* (Paris, 1510). Text of this plate, *Emendatio Vitae*, sig. A, iii.).

Written in the mid fifteenth century. An inscription on fol. iii records that 'Iste liber Constat Domino Ricardo Wydeuill' Comit' le Ryviers Et dominus (*sic*) de Wymington'. This probably refers to the first Earl who was created Earl Rivers in 1466, and who died in 1469. The stylistic features of this hand are similar to those of the hand of the Grant of Arms to the Tallow Chandlers' Company, dated 1456.

Compare with the previous plate, and note the marked French influence upon this hand (*v.* p. xxii), evident in the change in the duct of the hand, which is now free from the constriction imposed by a Textura model. Note the mobility, the proportions of the hand, and the continental version of the short **r** form (8, 'retinent').

demonum que maxime in cibo et potu hominibus | insidiantur. et eos decipiunt·/ effugabis. Aut enim | incautos per inmoderatam assumpcionem alimen-|torum ab arce virtutum deiciunt·/ aut per nimiam ab-|stinenciam in ipsa virtute frangunt. Multi enim sunt | qui in edendo semper fluctuant. Vt aut minus aut | magis sumant continue et formam viuendi nun-|quam retinent·/ Dum nunc hoc. nunc illud melius pu-|tant. Estimant enim insipientes et indocti qui | dulcedinem amoris Cristi nunquam experti sunt. quod |

(ii). **First quarter of the sixteenth century.** Oxford: Bodleian Library, MS. Arch. Selden B. 10 (*SC.* 3356), fol. 205^{r}.

A collection of excerpts from the works of John Lydgate entitled 'The Proverbs upon the Fall of Princes' (*v.* H. Bergen, *Lydgate's Fall of Princes*, part iv, E.E.T.S. (E.S.), 124, p. 123). Lines 1–6 of this plate are from *Fall of Princes*, Book V, lines 2531–6; lines 7–17 of this plate are from Lydgate's poem 'Consulo quisquis eris' (*Index*, 1294; ed. H. N. McCracken, *Minor Poems of Lydgate*, ii, E.E.T.S. (O.S.), 192, p. 750), lines 1–11.

The manuscript was copied in the first quarter of the sixteenth century from the printed edition of Wynkyn de Worde, 1519 (fol. 209^{v}, 'Here endeth the prouerbes of Lydgate vpon the fall of prynces. Enpryntede at London in fletestret at the sygne of the sonne by Wynkyn Worde'), *v.* Bergen, op. cit. The arms of the Percy family appear in an initial on fol. 197^{r}. The hand illustrated here also appears in another manuscript which belonged to the Percy family, Brit. Mus. Royal MS. 18 D ii. On evidence afforded by the contents, H. L. D. Ward dates the manuscript *c.* 1520 (*v.* Ward, *Cat. Romances*, i, p. 81).

The proportions of this hand, the structure of the letter forms, and the style of calligraphy betray the influence of the French '*Lettre Bastarde*'. Broken strokes forming the lobes of letters have been replaced by calligraphically formed curves, e.g. in **a** (5, 'hatefull'), and **d** (10, 'prudence'), but this is not consistent, and the calligraphy is not maintained throughout. Note the exaggeration of horns, especially on the tops of **e** and **s** (4, 'noblenes'), the calligraphic formation of **t** (5, 'there'), and the calligraphic treatment of descenders. Note also the occasional simple ascender (4, 'approch' 5, 'there'), cf. Pl. 13 (i).

Haue gouernaunce of all worldly ryches.
Agayne folke vnkynde loke that ye dysdayne.
Suffre them not haue non interesse.
For to approch to youre hygh noblenes.
For there ys no vyce more hatefull to conclude
Than is the vyce of ingratitude.

Consulo quisquis eris·/ qui pacis federa queris.
Consonus esto lupis·/ cum quibus esse cupis.

I Counsayll what so euyr thou be.
Of polycye/ foresyght and prudence.
If thou wylt lyue in peace and vnyte.
Co*n*forme thy selfe ⁊ thynke on this sentence.
Where so euer thou holde resydence.
Amonge wolles/ be wolwyshe of courage.
Lyon with lyons. a lambe for Innocence.
Lyke the audyence. so vtter thy language.

The vnycorne is caught withe maydens songe.

PLATES 16–18. The Handwriting of University Scribes

16 (i). **End of the thirteenth century.** Oxford: Bodleian Library, MS. Digby 55, fol. 146r.

'Questiones in Priscianum Minorem' (*v.* J. Pinborg, 'Die Entwicklung der Sprachtheorie im Mittelalters', *Beiträge zur Geschichte der Philosophie und Theologie des Mittelalters*, Bd. xlii, Heft 2 (1967), p. 93). 'Priscianus Minor' was the name given in the Middle Ages to Books xvii and xviii of the *Institutiones Grammaticae* of Priscianus Caesariensis.

Written towards the end of the thirteenth century (Pinborg, loc. cit., implies a date *c.* 1285 for the text). The nature of the text presupposes a university scribe.

Typical example of the cursive handwriting found in university books at this time (cf. F. Ehrle and P. Liebaert, *Specimina codicum latinorum Vaticanorum* (Berlin, 1932), no. 40). The handwriting is smaller and more compressed than that in the legal text in Pl. 1 (i), the strokes are much finer, and the scribe makes much more extensive use of abbreviations. Note the frequent appearance of headless **a** which is common in the smaller Textura book hands (*v.* Pl. 16 (ii)). Note that the loop to the right of ascenders begins about halfway up the ascender (b, 3, 'alterius') (*v.* note to Pl. 1 (i)). The common mark of abbreviation is frequently attached to the final letter of a word, thus resembling the *-er*, *-re* sign (a, 9, 'autem', 'esse').

Note the drastic abbreviation of technical terms which would occur frequently in such a text, e.g. a, 2, 'nomen'; a, 7, 'vocatiuo'; a, 12, 'persona'.

(col. a, ll. 1–16) sub proprietate 3^{e} si igitur debeat ista maxima confu-|sio vitari. ex suppositione huius necessarium est nomen vnius | esse persone. set diceret aliquis quod ex hoc non probatur | quod nomen debeat esse tantum 3^{e} magis quam prime | si igitur omnia nomina essent prime persone vitaretur bene | istud inconueniens. sicut sub proprietate 3^{e} et item secundum | dicta non deberet esse secunde persone nominatiuum in vocatiuo casu. | Ad primum dicendum. quod prima et secunda presentes sunt. quod | autem se habet ut istud de quo est sermo potest esse | presens uel absens. et eciam cum multe sunt qualitates | generales. et speciales. et singulis. qualibet singula reddun-|tur nomina. quare maior est confusio in 3^{a} persona quam in | prima uel secunda. quare nomina cum sint confusa et 3^{a} | persona confusa. cesserunt nomina in 3^{am} personam sibi aptam. | vt dicit priscianus. // ad aliud dicendum. quod modi significandi nominatiui | est causa quare nomina in vocatiuo casu non sunt 3^{e} persone.

(col. b, ll. 1–16) appositi. quia quedam proporcionalis. quedam similitudinis proporcionis. | quando vnus modus significandi in supposito corespondet modo in | apposito alterius racionis. ut modo casus et modus fieri modo per-|manentis. isti modi non sunt similes set proporcionales conueni-|entia similitudinis est inter modos significandi similes ut | est conuenientia inter personam appositi et personam suppositi. et numeri | ad numerum. isti enim modi tam in [proposito] supposito quam | in apposito sunt vnius racionis credo causam per quam utro-|bique non est vnius racionis quod quando duo constructibilia construitur (*for* construuntur) | ad inuicem per suos modos significandi necesse est v-|num modum significandi habere racionem dependentis et reliquum racionem | adiacentis sicut in re construitur cum apposito per personam su-|am. et appositum cum supposito per personam suam. ergo persona vnius | habet dependenciam racionem dependentis et reliqua racionem terminantis | ex hoc arguitur terminus et terminabile vniuersaliter non sunt vnius | racionis. comm(entator) super 6 phisicorum.

(ii). **Mid fourteenth century.** Oxford: Merton College, MS. O. 2. 1 (Coxe, 285), fol. 217r, col. b.

Albertus Magnus, 'De Nutrimento et Nutribili, Tractatus 1' (Thorndike and Kibre, 365; ed. P. Jammy, *Alberti Magni Opera Omnia* (Lyons, 1651), tom v. p. 175). On the manuscript *v.* Powicke, *MBMC.*, no. 389. The text of this manuscript is very corrupt.

Written in the mid fourteenth century by John Wylliott, Fellow of Merton College 1338–48, Chancellor of the University of Oxford in 1349 (fol. 220r, 'Explicit liber de nutrimento et nutrito Iohannes Wyliot'). On Wylliott *v.* Emden, *BRUO.*, and Powicke, op. cit.

This is not a cursive hand, but an example of the typical university book hand of the second half of the thirteenth and first half of the fourteenth centuries (*v.* J. Destrez, *La Pecia dans les mss. universitaires du xiiie et du xive siècle* (Paris, 1935)). It is a form of debased Textura (*v.* p. xiii). It is included here, first because it illustrates the capacity of an Oxford Master to write a book hand, and secondly because of the influence this kind of handwriting had upon the development of Anglicana Formata. Note the forms of **r** (9, 'declarare') and **s** (10, 'habentes'), which passed into Anglicana Formata. The headless **a** (10, 'actiue') is found in thirteenth-century Anglicana (Pls. 1 (i); 16 (i)).

For an example of the cursive handwriting (Anglicana) of another Fellow of Merton about this time, Simon Bredon, *v.* the facsimile in R. T. Gunther, *Early Science in Oxford*, ii, O.H.S. lxxviii (1923), p. 52.

(ll. 1–24) (D)E ANIMA. secundum seipsam in pre| cedenti libro dictum est. set quia non | tantum secundum seipsam querimus cong|noscere animam. set et opera eius et passio|nes. et ea que circa operatur et a quibus | passionem recipit propriam ideo iterum quasi | a principio incipientes de ipsa opera | eius que actiuis suis agit potenciis | declarare intendimus. Diximus autem in libro de anima quod | actiue potencie nichil similitudinis et passiuis habentes | sunt nutritiua. ⌜et⌝ augmentatiua. et generatiua que eciam secundum naturam | sunt prime eo quod speculacio naturalis incipit a magis communi | et deuenit et (*for* in) particulare determinatum magis enim commune phisice sump|tum eciam secundum nos prius est sicut sepe ostendimus. Et | ideo de hiis operacionibus anime in hunc librum speculatiuum (*for* in hoc libro speculabimur). Quia | uero obiectum preiacet operi ideo oportet agere de nutrimento quia | ex racione illius sciemus opera nutricionis. Nos autem iam osten|dimus quod nutrimentum et angues (*for* augens). et ex quo est generacio | idem est omnino. set esse alterum est et ideo tribus operibus qui sunt | nutrire augere generare idem subicitur circa quod operantur et ex | quo oportet anima (*for* omnia) hec tria opera cognoscere // queremus igitur et quid | est quod nutret et auget. et generat. et cuius est nutrimentum | proprie et quomodo est et qua de causa. et usque ad quem terminum. | et supponemus omnia que in libro perygeneseos.

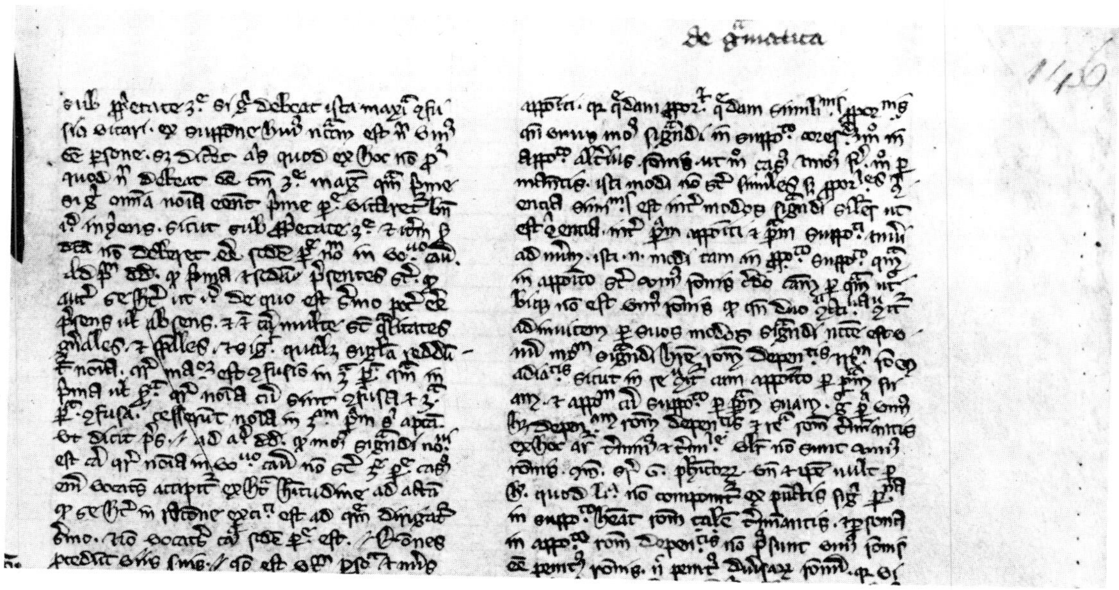
De gramatica

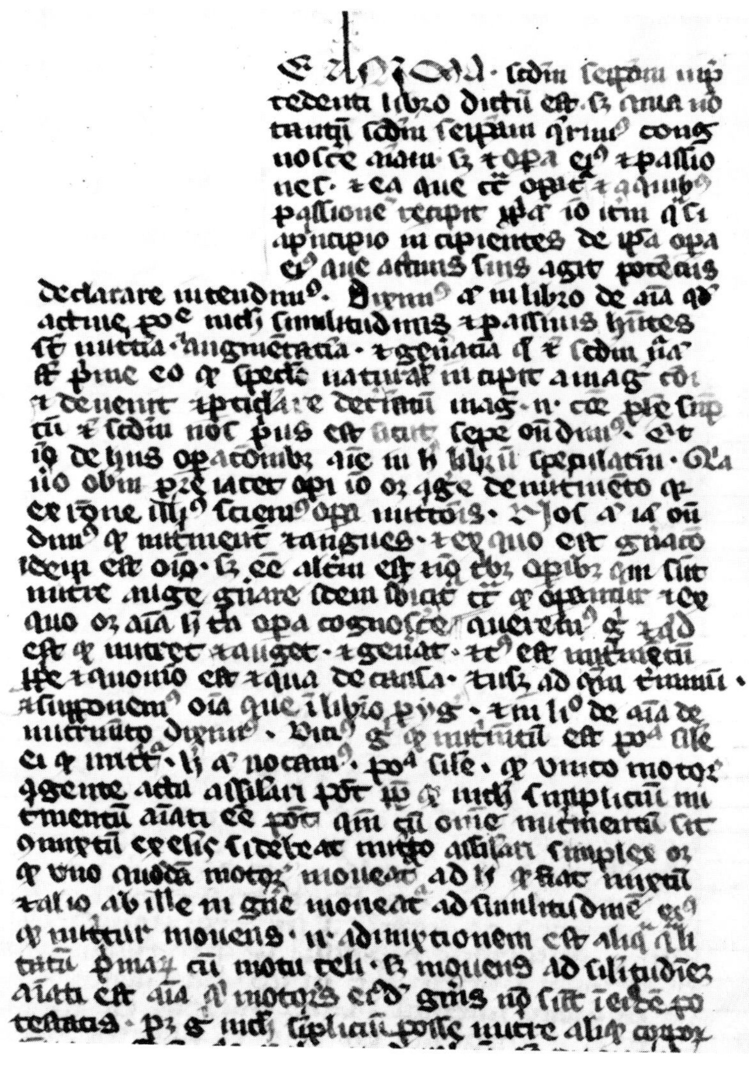

.21.

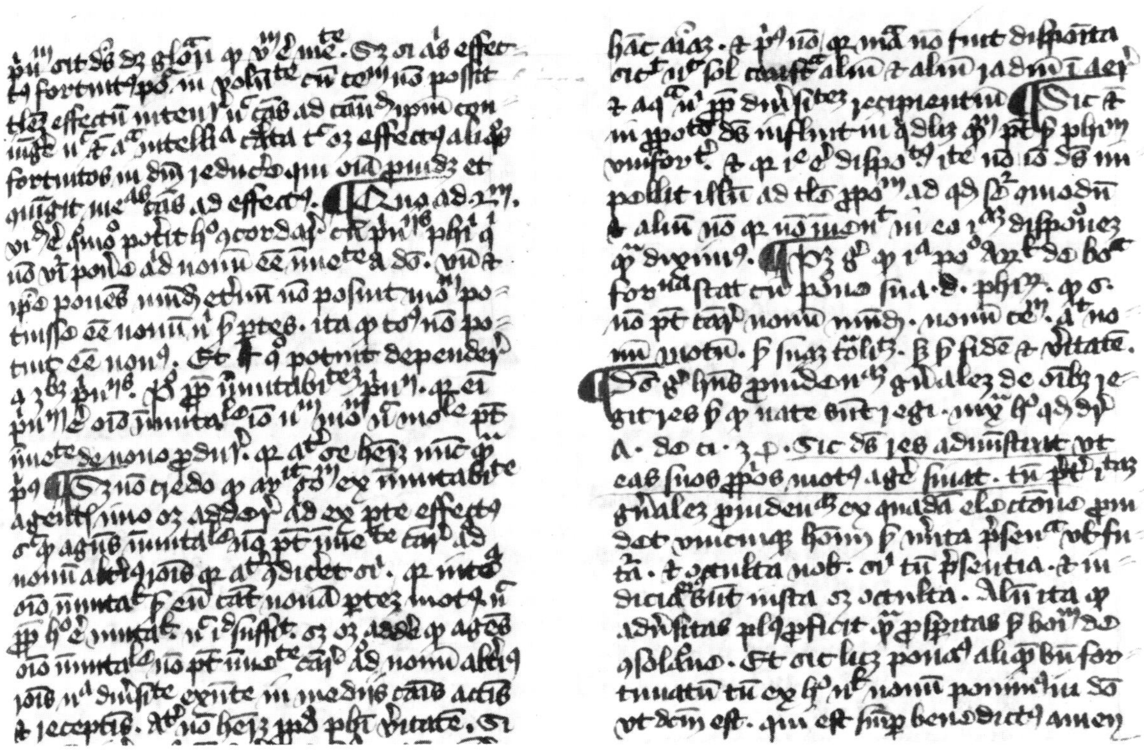

.142.

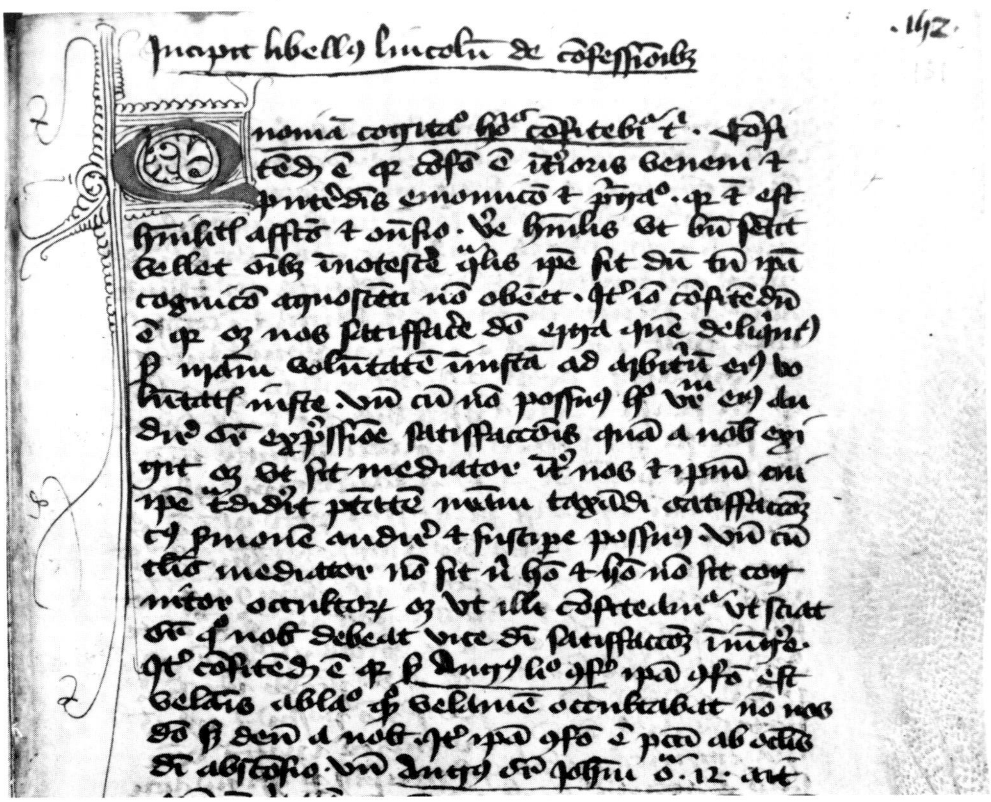

Incipit libellus lincoln de confessionibus

17 (i). 1429. Cambridge: University Library, MS. Ff. 3. 27, fol. 45^r^.

'Quaestiones Quodlibetales Iohannis Duns Scoti per Iohannem Sharpe Abbreviatae'. (On Sharpe *v.* Emden, *BRUO.*)

Written in Oxford in 1429 (fol. 45^r, '. . . et manu [ ] scripta . . . Scriptus fuit liber iste Anno Domini. M^o^ C^o^C^o^C^o^C^o^ xx^o^ ix^o^ in Oxonia.' The name of the scribe has been erased and is not legible under ultra-violet light.).

Typical Oxford hand of the period 1425–50. It is such a skilful blend of Anglicana (cf. Pls. 2 (ii); 3 (i)) and Secretary that the influence of the latter is not immediately obvious, except in the direction of the minim strokes, and in the presence of Secretary graphs, especially **r** (a, 2, 'fortuitus') and **s** (a, 9, 'ponens'). The treatment of ascenders and descenders is typical of current Anglicana. The hand is compact and upright without trace of splay, or of the horns which are usually characteristic of such a well-written hand at this time (cf. Pls. 2 (ii); 11 (ii)). Note the survival of the headless **a** form (cf. Pl. 16 (i)).

(col. a) principium sit deus debet glosari quod verum est mediate. Set si aliquis effec-|tus fortuitus ponitur in voluntate cum celum non possit | talem effectum intendere nec causas ad causandum ipsum con-|iungere nec eciam aliqua intelligencia creata tunc oportet effectus aliquos | fortuitos in deum reducere qui omnia prouidet et | coniungit medias causas ad effectus. ¶ Quoad .2^m^. | videndum est quomodo poterit hoc concordare cum principiis phisici qui | non videtur ponere aliquid nouum esse immediate a deo. vnde et | ipse ponens mundum eternum non posuit motum po-|tuisse esse nouum nisi secundum partes. ita quod totus non po-|tuit esse nouus. Et [hec] conclusio potuit dependere | a tribus principiis. Primo propter immutabilitatem principii. quia enim | principium est omnino immutabile ideo nullum motum nec mobile potest | immediate de nouo producere. quia aliter se haberet nunc quam | prius ¶ Set non credo quod arguit solum ex immutabilitate | agentis imo oportet addere aliquid ex parte effectus | sic quod agens immutabile non potest immediate causare aliquod | nouum alterius rationis quia aliter contradiceret sibi. quia intelligencia | omnino immutabilis secundum eum causat nouam partem motus. nec | propter hoc est mutabilis. nec istud sufficit. set oportet addere quod agens | omnino immutabile non potest immediate causare aliquod nouum alterius | rationis nulla diuersitate existente in mediis causis actiuis | et receptiuis. Aliter non haberet propositio phisici veritatem. si |

(col. b) hanc animam. et prius non/ quia materia non fuit disposita | sicut nec sol causat alium et alium radium in aere | et aqua nisi propter diuersitatem recipientium ¶ Sic eciam | in propositio deus influit in quidlibet quantum potest secundum phisicum | vniformiter. et quia iste est dispositus. iste non ideo deus im-|pellit illum ad tale propositum ad quod sequitur commodum | et alium non quia non inuenit in eo illam dispositionem | quam diximus. ¶ Patet igitur quod ista positio Aristotelis de bona | fortuna stat cum positione sua .8. phisicorum quod scilicet | non potest causare nouum mundum. nouum celum. aut no-|uum motum. secundum suam totalitatem. set secundum fidem et veritatem. | ¶ Deus igitur habens prouidenciam generalem de omnibus re-|git res secundum quod nate sunt regi. iuxta hoc quod dicitur | 7. de ciuitate dei .30. **sic deus res administrat vt** | **eas suos proprios motus agere sinat. tamen** preter istam | generalem prouidentiam ex quadam electione proui-|det vnicuique hominum secundum merita presentia vel fu-|tura. et occulta nobis. sibi tamen presentia. et iu-|dicia ⌜eius⌝ sunt iusta set occulta. Aliquando ita quod | aduersitas plus proficit quam prosperitas secundum boitium de | consolacione. Et sic licet ponamus aliquem bene for-|tunatum tamen ex hoc nichil nouum ponimus in deo vt dictum est. qui est semper benedictus amen |

(ii). Mid fifteenth century. Oxford: Bodleian Library, MS. Bodley 52 (*SC.* 1969), fol. 151^r^.

The 'libellus Lincolniensis de confessionibus' is one of the sermons of Robert Grosseteste (S. Harrison Thomson, *The Writings of Robert Grosseteste* (Cambridge, 1940), p. 172, no. 15). The manuscript contains a collection of miscellaneous theological and ecclesiastical pieces which 'illustrate the interests of a Merton Fellow in the fifteenth century' (Powicke, *MBMC.*, p. 207, no. 974).

Written in Oxford towards the end of the second quarter of the fifteenth century by John Maynesford, Fellow of Merton College 1429–40 (fol. 59^r, 'Et Deo gratias quod Maynsforth'). On Maynesford *v.* Emden, *BRUO.*

This hand betrays stronger Secretary influence than that of the previous plate. There is more suggestion of splay, and the descenders of **f**, long-**s**, and **p**, although upright, are more tapered than those in the earlier hand (cf. 10, 'possumus', and made more currently, 6, 'sit'). Anglicana graphs appear only occasionally, e.g. **r** (9, 'arbitrium') and **s** (5, 'affectus').

Incipit libellus lincolniensis de confessionibus Quoniam cogitacio hominis confitebitur tibi. Confi|tendum est quia confessio est interioris veneni et | putredinis euomicio[1] et purgacio. quia eciam est | humilitatis affectus et ostensio. Vere humilis vt bene sentit | vellet omnibus innotescere qualis ipse sit dum tamen ipsa | cognicio agnoscenti non obesset. Item ideo confitendum | est quia oportet nos satisfacere deo erga quem deliquimus | secundum nostram voluntatem iniustam ad arbitrium eius vo|luntatis iuste. Vnde cum non possumus hoc verbum eius au|dire super expressione satisfaccionis quam a nobis exi|git oportet vt sit mediator inter nos et ipsum cui | ipse tradiderit potestatem nostram taxandi satisfaccionem | cuius sermonem audire et suscipere possumus. Vnde cum | talis mediator non sit nisi homo et homo non sit cog|nitor occultorum oportet vt illi confiteamur vt sciat | super quo nobis debeat vice dei satisfaccionem iniungere. | Item confitendum est quia secundum **Augustinum libro confessionum** ipsa confessio est | velaminis ablatio quod velamen occultabat non nos | deo set deum a nobis. Item ipsa confessio est peccati ab oculis | dei absconsio. Vnde **Augustinus super Iohannem omelia .12.** ait |

[1] The scribe originally wrote 'emomicio' and subsequently erased the first minim of the first **m**.

18 (i). 1467. Oxford: New College, MS. 305, fol. 104r.

John Felton, 'Sermones Dominicales' (*v.* Emden, *BRUO.*).

Written by Thomas Holme in 1467 (fol. 146r, erased inscription legible under ultra-violet light 'Iste liber scriptus est apud Wrytell (i.e. Writtle, Essex) per manum Magistri Thome Holme. Anno Domini Mmo CCCCmo sexagesimo septimo . . .').

Compare with previous plate and note closer resemblance of this hand to contemporary Secretary (cf. Pls. 12 (ii); 13 (i)). Note the proportions of the hand; the more pronounced splay (e.g. a, 9); and despite the currency of the hand, the emphasis upon superficial details of style, particularly the horns on the letters, e.g. **e** (a, 10, 'existentem') and '2'-shaped **r** (a, 2, 'hora'). Note also the increase in the number of otiose strokes even in this current hand, e.g. after final **t** (a, 1, 'sunt', b, 9, 'concedat').

(col. a) horis canonicis sunt finiende. In matutino | laudatur. quia illa hora Cristus natus est | Iuda traditus. a Iudeis captus illusus | et ad iudicium creditur venturus iuxta illud | Matthei .25. Media nocte clamor factus est .et cetera. | In hora prima deus laudatur quia tunc celum | et terram ad nostrum seruicium creauit. et tunc ad | templum ire personaliter consueuit. iuxta illud | luce .21. Omnis populi manecabant (*for* populus manecabat). id est mane | veniebant ad ipsum in templo existentem | Mulieribus eciam post resurreccionem in hac apparuit | hora. In tercia hora laudatur. quia tunc Cristus ad | columpnam flagellatus fuit. et sentenciam sue | mortis accepit. In hora sexta. laudatur. | quia tunc Cristus in cruce fuit crucifixus et sol ob|scuratus. Cristus eciam volens ascendere in celum | cum discipulis fuit conuiuatus. In hora nona. |

(col. b) tacere. Ieremie .28. Factus est sermo domini in corde | meo quasi ignis estuans clausus in ossibus meis. | et defeci ferre non sustinens. Per hoc quod tin|tinabula erant in fine tunice. significatur finalis | perseuerancia. sine qua nulla bona sunt deo | accepta. Bernardus. Tolle perseueranciam nec ob|sequium mercedem habet. nec beneficium gratiam. nec lau|dem fortitudo. set qui perseuerauerit usque in finem | hic saluus erit. hoc concedat nobis omnibus Cristus | AmeN |
(o)Mnis qui se exaltat humiliabitur | et cetera. luce .18. Carissimi. si quis spargeret | aurum et argentum uel lapides preciosas. qui|libet vestrum respiceret et manum apponeret | et colligeret quantum posset. Set ego non spargo | vobis huiusmodi. set preciosiora scilicet verba domini. | et hoc patet tam racione quam exemplo. Primo racione sic. |

(ii). 1491/2. Oxford: University College, MS. 156, fol. 1r.

'Excerpta ex opere De Sacramentalibus Thomae Waldensis per Iohannem Russell collecta' (fol. vii, 'Ego Iohannes Russell episcopus Lincolniensis fatigatus hoc anno 1491 oxonie cum multis hereticis postquam pervenit in manus meas liber fratris Thome Waldensis . . . contra Wicleuistas . . . cogitaui aliqua excerpere ex eodem libro super sacramentalibus in que Lollardi ipsi maxime invehuntur . . .'). On Thomas Netter (Waldensis) *v.* Emden, *BRUO.*

Written by John Russell in 1491/2 (fol. vii, 'Iohanne Lincolniensis manu propria in festo epiphanie apud Woborn anno 1491 secundum computacionem ecclesie Anglicane'). On Russell, Fellow of New College 1449–62, Chancellor of the University of Oxford 1483–94, etc. *v.* Emden, *BRUO.*

The kind of handwriting which had been developed in the universities has become submerged in a highly current, personal style. On the one hand Russell's ability to write a humanist hand is reflected here in the presence of humanist forms: e.g. the treatment of ascenders, and the form of **g** in 4, 'excogitare'. On the other hand the extreme currency of the hand distorts the familiar letter forms found in the previous plate: e.g. the **e** in 4, 'poterant', and the minims which have been reduced almost to dots on the line of writing (6, 'inhibuit').

¶ Ex epistula ⌜fratris⌝ Thome Waldensis ad papam martinum Vtum in prefacione | sua ad opus de sacramentalibus. Habetur quod licitum est in confutacione | heresum ipsas pretitulare. quamuis aliqui velint contrarium ⌜precauentes⌝ ne ita discant | innocentes. quod excogitare non poterant[1] Sed grauius/ inquit/ multum esset | si non essent moniti vnde fugerent innocentes. Numquid non erat tunc innocens prothoplaustus cum ostenderet ei deus lignum cuius esum inhibuit? | At iterum aiunt in huiusmodi pretitulacione/ heresum videretur plurimum honorari. | Sed legant origenem omelia .ixa. super illo loco numeri xvi. quo sediciosa | turribula mandantur produci in laminas et altari affigi. Ista inquit | uatilla erea id est hereticorum voces adhibeamus ad altare dei. vbi diuinus | ignis est. vbi vera fidei predicatio/ melius ipsa veritas ex falsorum | comparatione fulgebit. ¶ Idcirco cuius doctrina catholicam contra |

[1] Heading in margin (only partly visible on plate), '**¶ Quod satius es(t confutendas) | hereses pre(titulare quam) | ipsas tace(ndo sinere) | innocentes (in ipsas improuisos) | incidere**'.

xli

horis canonicis sunt fruende. In matutino
laudatur quia illa hora Christus natus est
Iuda tradente a Iudeis captus illusus
et ad mortem queritur. Veterumque magistri illud
Matthei 25. Media nocte clamor factus est. etc.
In hora prima deus laudatur quia tunc Christus
pro ham ad verum fructum [illegible]. et tunc ad
templum ire personaliter consueverunt. magister illud
Luce 21. Omnis populus manicabat. i. mane
veniebant ad ipsum in templo existentem
mulieribus et post resurrectionem in hac apparuit
hora. In tercia hora laudatur. quia tunc est ad
columpnam flagellatus fuit. et sinam sui
mortis accepit. In hora sexta laudatur
quia tunc etc. in qua fuit quasi ... et solos
fructus. etc. et volens ascendere in celum
cum discipulis fuit ... In hora nona.

tate. Ieremie 20. Factus est sermo domini in corde
meo quasi ignis estuans claususque in ossibus meis.
et defeci ferre non sustinens. Quod hoc quia tu
tabula erant in sic tunde. Sequitur fidelis
perseverancia. sine qua nulla bona fuit deo
accepta. Bernardus. Tolle perseveranciam nec ob
sequium mercedem habet. nec beneficium gratiam. nec laus
de fortitudo. Sed qui perseveravit usque in finem
hic salvus erit. hoc concedat nobis omnibus etc.
Amen 2.2

Omnis qui se exaltat humiliabitur
etc. Luce 18. Carissimi. si quis preferet
aurum et argentum vel lapides preciosos. quilibet
libet eorum respiceret et manum apponeret
et colligeret quantum possit. Set ego non prefero
vobis huiusmodi. sed preciosiora. scilicet verba domini.
et hoc propter tres raciones quia etc. Prima racione sic.
Omnis thesaurus mundi. sive auri sive ar

Excepta [illegible] Thome walden ad papam martinum vtum in prefacione
sua ad opus de sacramentalibus. Habet quod licitum est in confutacione
hereticorum. ipsorum postulare. [illegible] aliquam velut [illegible] [illegible] ne ita distant
[illegible]. quod excogitare non poterant. Sed gravius [illegible] esset
si non essent [illegible] unde fugerent [illegible]. [illegible] erat tunc
[illegible] [illegible] ostenderet ei [illegible] legendi [illegible]
[illegible] sub huius postulacionem [illegible] videretur [illegible] honorari.
Sed legerunt origenem omelia [illegible] super illo loco [illegible] quo preciosa
turibula mandantur [illegible] in laminas et altare affigi. Ista [illegible]
[illegible] i. [illegible] adhibeamus ad altare dei. ubi [illegible]
[illegible] est. ubi vera fidei [illegible] [illegible] veritas ex falsorum
comparacione fulgebit. [illegible] eius doctrinam catholicam contra

[illegible] sacrum est
heresis [illegible]
ipsorum [illegible]
[illegible]
[illegible]

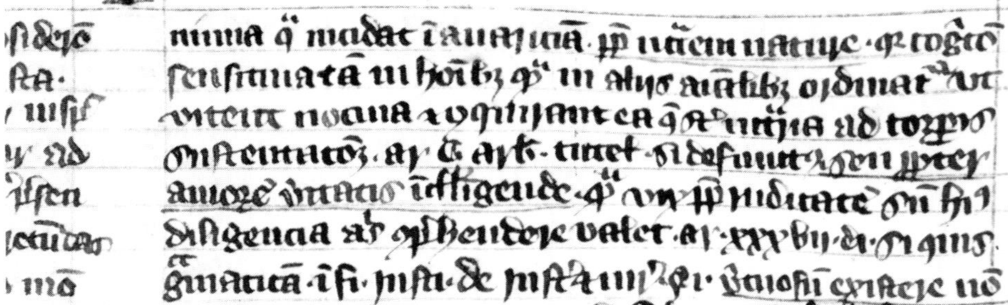

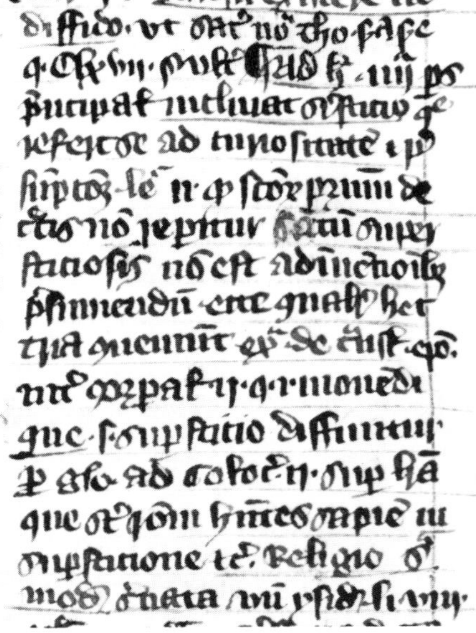

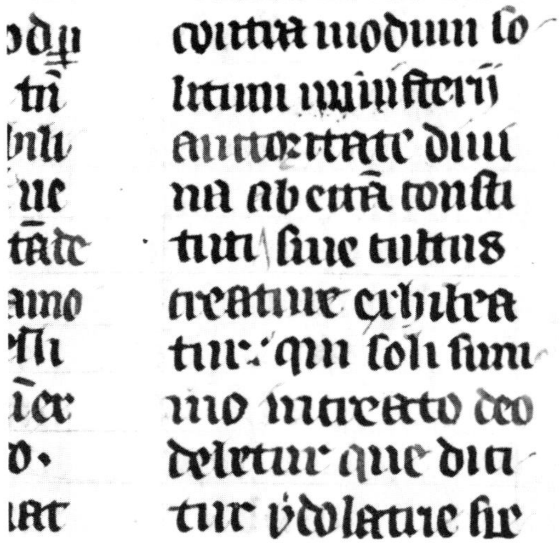

contra modum so litum ministerij auctoritate diui na ab ecclesia consti tuti sine cultus creature exhibea tur: qui soli sum mo increato deo debetur que dici tur ydolatrie sic

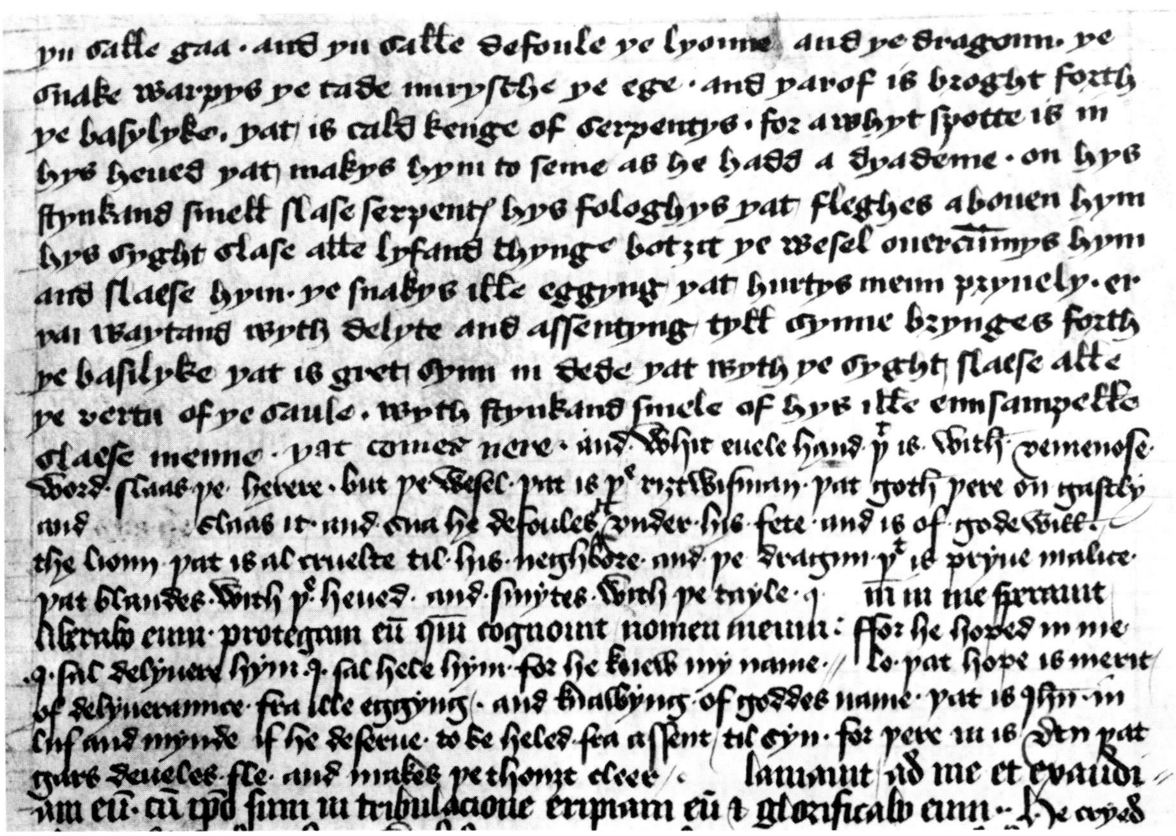

yu salle gaa · and yu salle defoule ye lyoune and ye dragoun · ye snake warpys ye tade imyssche ye ege · and yarof is broght forth ye basylyke · yat is cald kenge of serpentys · for a whyt spotte is in hys heued yat makys hym to seme as he hadd a dyademe · on hys stynkand smelt slase serpentys hys fologhys yat fleghes aboune hym hys syght slase alle lyfand thynge botzet ye wesel ouercomys hym and slaese hym · ye snakys ilke eggyng yat hurtys mem pryuely · er yai waytand wyth delyte and assentyng tyll synne bryngeS forth ye basilyke yat is ded synne in dede yat wyth ye syght slaese alle ye vertu of ye saule · wyth stynkand smele of hys ilke ensampelle slaese menne · yat comes nere · and whit euele hand yt is with venenose word · slaas ye heuere · but ye wesel · yat is ye rightwisman · yat goth yere on gastly and slaas it · and sua he defoules vnder his fete and is of gode wille · the lioun yat is al cruelte til his neghbore · and ye dragun yt is pryue malice yat blawes with ye heued · and smytes with ye tayle · q in me sperauit liberabo eum · protegam eu qm cognouit nomen meum: ffor he hopes in me I sal deliuere hym · I sal hele hym · for he knew my name · // To yat hope is merit of deliueraunce · fra ilke eggyng · and knawyng of goddes name · yat is ihū · in lif and mynde if he deserue to be heled · fra assent til syn · for yere it is doun yat gares deueles fle · and makes ye thornz clere · Clamauit ad me et exaudi am eu · cu ipso sum in tribulacione eripiam eu et glorificabo eum · · He cryed

PLATES 19–20. Developments in the Hierarchy of Scripts

19 (i). 1355. Cambridge: Gonville and Caius College, MS. 282/675, fol. 25^{r}, col. b.

John of Acton, 'Septuplum cum commentario' (*v.* Emden, *BRUO.*).

Written in 1355 by Edmund de Multon (fol. 140^{v}, 'Scriptus extitit xvii kal. Aug. a.d. millesimo ccc l^{mo} quinto ab Edmundo de Multon sacerdote et istius libri primo possessore').

The scribe has used Textura Semi-quadrata for the text and Anglicana Formata for the commentary, thus illustrating the relative position of the two scripts in the hierarchy of scripts. Note how the text is placed centrally and the commentary is written around it, a layout common in the thirteenth and fourteenth centuries, but not so common later (cf. Pl. 20 (i)).

In the commentary note the method of abbreviation in the citations of legal sources, which is peculiar to legal texts. The form of the citation here is as follows: it is introduced by 'ar.' (= argumento); this is followed by the sigla indicating the collection, then the rubric of the *titulus*, then the incipit of the *lex* or *canon* or *capitulum*, and then, if required, by the paragraph too. Thus in line 4 the reference is to *Codex Iustiniani*, Liber V, Tit. 51 (rubric: 'Arbitrium tutelae'), 10 (incipit: 'Si defunctus'). (For a fuller account of this practice *v.* H. Kantorowicz, 'Die Allegationen im späteren Mittelalter', *Archiv für Urkundenforschung*, xiii (1935), 15–29.)

(*Commentary*) nimia qua incidat in auariciam. **propter necessitatem nature.** quia cognicio | sensitiua tam in hominibus quam in aliis animalibus ordinatur vt | vitent nociua et conquirant ea que sunt necessaria ad corporis | sustentacionem. argumento Codice arbitrium tutelae. si defunctus.[1] **seu propter** | **amorem veritatis intelligende.** quam vix propter ruditatem sine huiusmodi | diligencia aliquis comprehendere valet. argumento .xxxvii. distinctione. si quis grammaticam.[2] in fine. Institucionum. de Iusticia et iure § .i.[3] **virtuosum existere non** | **diffido.** vt satis notat .Thomas. secunda secunde | questione. Clxvii. § vltima ¶ **Ad hec** quarta pars | principalis **inclinat superstitio** que | refert se ad curiositatem et pre|sumpcionem. legitur enim quod sanctorum patrum de|cretis non reperitur sancitum super|sticiosis non est adinuentionibus | presumendum. ecce qualiter hec | tria conueniunt. extra de translacione episcopo (*for* episcopi). | inter corporalia.[4] ii. q .i. mouendi | **que** scilicet superstício diffinitur | per glosam ad Colocenses .ii. super littera | que sunt racionem habentes sapiencie in supersticione et cetera. **Religio supra** | **modum seruata** vnde ysidorus libro .viii. |

(*Text*) contra modum so-|litum ministerii | auctoritate diui|na ab ecclesia consti|tuti[5] siue cultus | creature exhibea|tur.·/ qui soli sum-|mo increato deo | debetur que dici-|tur ydolatrie spe|

[1] *Codex* V. Tit. 51. 10.
[2] *Decretum* I. Dist. xxxvii. c. x.
[3] *Institutiones* I. i. Tit. 1.
[4] *Decretalium* I. Tit. vii. cap. ii.
[5] Caret mark inserted.

(ii). First half of the fifteenth century. Oxford: Bodleian Library, MS. Bodley 467 (*SC.* 2487) fol. 120^{r}.

The English commentary of Richard Rolle on the Psalter with the Latin text as lemmata (*v.* Allen, 1927, p. 171; ed. H. R. Bramley, *The Psalter by Richard Rolle of Hampole* (Oxford, 1884), text of this plate, ibid., p. 333).

Written in the first half of the fifteenth century (cf. the hand of the second scribe (lines 11–21) with Pls. 10 (i), and 11 (ii)). The book belonged to Hugo Eyton subprior of S. Albans (fol. 171, 'Iste liber est domini Hugonis Eyton supprioris monasterii Sancti Albani . . .').

For his commentary, the first scribe (lines 1–11) has used a mixed hand of a kind which is very common in vernacular manuscripts of this period. It is based upon Anglicana Formata (note especially the duct; the direction of the independent minim strokes, cf. Pl. 6 (i); the shape of the descenders; and the forms of **d** and **g**), but contains the Secretary forms of **a**, **r**, and **s**. Although not illustrated here, he has used a form of Textura for the lemmata, which is similar to that used in the previous plate. The second scribe (lines 11–21) has used Secretary for the commentary and early Bastard Secretary for the lemmata (lines 15 and 20). Thus the hierarchy of scripts has a parallel in a hierarchy of varieties of the Secretary script.

The hand of the first scribe contains a number of interesting features. The hairline through **ll** is clearly otiose since in many cases he adds final -e (1, 'salle'). **þ** and **y** are indistinguishable. He uses suprascript **e** as an abbreviation to indicate the ending of the northern form of the third person singular present indicative (2, 'nurysch*es*'), and the plural of a noun (6 'thyng*es*').

(ll. 1–20) yu salle gaa. and yu salle defoule ye lyonne and ye dragonn. ye | snake warpys ye tade nurysch*es* ye ege. and yarof is broght forth | ye basylyke. yat is cald kenge of serpentys. for a whyt spotte is in | hys heued yat makys hym to seme as he hadd a dyademe. on hys | stynkand smell' slase serpentę hys fologhys (*for* fogholys) yat fleghes abouen hym | hys syght slase alle lyfand thyng*es* bot ȝit ye wesel ouercu*m*mys hym | and slaese hym. ye snakys ille eggyng yat hurtys menn pryuely. er | yai waytand wyth delyte and assentyng tyll' synne brynges forth | ye basilyke yat is gret synn in dede yat wyth ye syght slaese alle | ye vertu of ye saule . wyth stynkand smele of hys ille ennsampelle | slaese menne. yat comes nere.[1] and whit euele hand þ^{t} is with vemenose | word slaas þe herere. but þe wesel þat is þ^{e} riȝtwisman þat goth þere on gastly | and [ ] slaas it. and sua he defoules ⸢it⸣ vnder his fete and is of godewill'./ | the lioun þat is al cruelte til his neghbore and þe dragun þ^{t} is pryue malice. | þat blandes with þ^{e} heued and smytes with þe tayle.[2] (Q)ui in me sperauit | liberabo eum. protegam eum qui cognouit nomen meum.·/ For he hoped in me | I sal delyuere hym I sal hele hym for he knew my name.// lo þat hope is merit | of delyueraunce fra ille eggyng/. and knawyng of goddes name þat is Ih*es*u in | luf and mynde if he deserue to be heled fra assent/ til syn . for þere in is v*er*tu þat | gars deueles fle and makes þe thouȝt cleer/

[1] Change of hand.
[2] Lemmata in Bastard Secretary.

20 (i). Mid fifteenth century. Oxford: Bodleian Library, MS. Bodley 248 (*SC.* 2247), fol. 100^r (nine tenths actual size).

William Lyndwood, 'Provinciale, seu Constitutiones Anglie' (*v.* C. R. Cheney, 'William Lyndwood's *Provinciale*', *The Jurist*, xxi (1961), pp. 405–34). On Lyndwood, *v.* Emden, *BRUC.* and *BRUO.* Printed at Oxford, 1679; text of this plate, ibid., pp. 75–6.

Written in the mid fifteenth century (the text was completed by Lyndwood in 1434 which provides a *terminus post quem* for the manuscript).

The scribe has used Textura Quadrata (cf. Pl. 22 (ii)) for the text, a small clear Secretary for the commentary, and a somewhat current version of Bastard Secretary for the heading. Cf. with Pl. 19 (i), and note the difference in the layout.

For the method of abbreviation peculiar to the citations in legal texts *v.* note to Pl. 19 (i). In addition note here the citations to the glossators (usually introduced by 'ut notatur'). On the glossators *v.* J. F. von Schulte, *Die Geschichte der Quellen und Literatur des canonischen Rechts* (Stuttgart, 1875–7), and A. van Hove, *Prolegomena* (Antwerp, 1945).

(col. a) non autem antiqui declaracionem vt notatur de eleccione. capitulo prou-|ida[1] eodem verbo per Cardinalem et Archidiaconum .libro vi^o. et circa hoc vide | notata per Iohannem Andree in prohemio clementinarum eodem verbo et eodem verbo per gesselinum et | per paulum/ nec semper hec diccio approbat ea que preces-|serunt. vt notat Willelmus de penitenciis et remissionibus[2] capitulo finali eodem verbo in clementinarum.| **permittatur** id est tolleretur. prout alias de hoc et multi-|plici significacione huius diccionis permittere. notatur .iii. distinctio omnis | autem lex[3] per Iohannem. vel dic permittatur id est concedatur. sicut alias | exponitur. de etate et qualitate capitulo vnico[4] per Cardinalem et Archidiaconum libro vi^o | **publice** ⌜id est⌝ coram iudice vel publice id est notorie vel palam | de vsuris. capitulo .i.[5] verbo publice per Archidiaconum libro vi^o. publice namque fieri | id dicitur quod omnibus patet. Digestum. de suspectis tutoribus. lege i. |§ consequens.[6] Set in hoc casu puto publice debere intelligi | respectu non solum Iudicis set fori seu Curie et multitu-|dinis ibi presencium. prout alias notatur in capitulo finali de vita et honestate | clericorum.[7] verbo publice per Willelmum in clementinarum. et sic publice dicitur coram populo | vel publice id est communiter coram multis. Ad quod vide notata | in constitucione otonis. licet verbo publice per Iohannem de atona. | **prius** scilicet antequam illud officium exerceat **per triennium.** de | iure ciuili limitatur quinquenium. vt patet in prohemio Digesti § set quia solitum.[8] et legitur et notatur. Codice de aduocatis diuersorum iudicum | lege iubemus.[9] Nec video quid moueret statuentem ad limita-|cionem minoris temporis nisi intelligas hoc. vt scilicet aliquis | aduocet in curiis pedaneis et inferioribus vbi non | tractantur cause graues set modici ponderis. In talibus | namque. sufficere videtur quod aliquis sit exercitatus in causis | et habeat practicam cum speculatiua per triennium vt hic et | facit ad hoc Codex. de Iudiciis lege certi iuris.[10] In curiis | tamen maioribus et in quibus tractantur ardue cause. opus | est aduocatis fultis maiori sciencia. vt dicta lege iubemus | cum concordanciis. **Audiuerit** vt discipulus sub magistro | siue doctore nec refert vt videtur an in studio generali. |

(col. b, ll. 1–20) nonicum et ciuile. **fidem** id est probacionem **testimonio.** scilicet | per testimonium doctoris sub quo studuit. Codex de aduocatis | diuersorum iudiciorum.[11] lege nemini circa medium[11]// Poterit eciam | in hoc casu sufficere littera testimonialis Cancellarii | Vniuersitatis in qua studuit. vel poterit hoc probare | per testes. **facti euidenciam.** quia positus ad examen | non est repertus habilis nec in iure peritus respectu tempor-|is triennii, **iuramento.** sic ergo sufficit ad effectum | quod permittatur publice postulare deficiente condigno | testimonio. vel facti euidencia. si iuret per triennium | se audiuisse ius canonicum et ciuile. cum debita | diligencia.// Set quero quid operabitur prestacio huius | iuramenti. cum per facti euidenciam apparet insuffi-|ciens. Dic quod operabitur ad hoc. vt per illud probet se per | triennium audiuisse iura. non tamen ad hoc. quod propterea | iudex teneatur eum admittere ad officium aduocan-|di. nam licet iudex prestito huiusmodi iuramento possit | eum admittere. non tamen ad hoc tenetur. quia non quicquid | iudicis potestati committitur iuris necessitati sup-|ponitur.

[1] *Sexti Decretalium* I. Tit. vi. cap. xliv.
[2] *Clementinarum* V. Tit. ix, 'De penitenciis et remissionibus'.
[3] *Decretum* I. Dist. iii. c. iv.
[4] *Sexti Decretalium* I. Tit. x.
[5] *Sexti Decretalium* V. Tit. v. cap. i.
[6] *Digest* XXVI. Tit. x. i, § 6.
[7] *Clementinarum* III. Tit. i.
[8] *Digest* Praefationes, I, 'Omnem reipublicae', § 5.
[9] *Codex* II. Tit. viii. 3.
[10] *Codex* III. Tit. i. 17.
[11] *Codex* II. Tit. vii.

(ii). c. 1553–8. Oxford: Bodleian Library, MS. Bodley 431 (*SC.* 2368), fol. 96^r.

S. Thomas More, 'Treatise on the Passion' (S. Gibson, *S. Thomas More, a Preliminary Bibliography* (New Haven, 1961), no. 73. Printed in *The Workes of Sir Thomas More* (London, 1557, *STC.* 18076), pp. 1270–1404, text of this plate, ibid., p. 1325, col. b). See C. Kirchberger, 'Bodleian MSS. relating to the spiritual life 1500–1700', *Bodleian Library Record*, iii (1950–1), p. 161.

Written in the mid sixteenth century. The presence of the words 'M. REGINA' in the ornamented initial on fol. 1^r, and of 'VOX POPULI VOX DEI VIVAT REGINA MARIA M.R.' in the ornamented initial on fol. 37^r indicates that the manuscript was probably written during the reign of Mary Tudor (1553–8).

Compare with the previous plates and note how the varieties of Secretary have replaced the other scripts. The scribe has used Bastard Secretary for the translation of the text, and Secretary for the commentary. Note the use of 'Italic' based on the humanist cursive for the Latin lemmata, a practice common in printed books of the time.

or Hic est calix nouum testamentum in meo sanguine, qui | pro vobis et pro multis fundetur in remissionem peccatorum, | This is the chalyce the newe testamente in | my bloude, which shalbe sheade for you and | for many for the remyssion of synnes. Here | you se that by the wordes of our Saviour rehearsed by | *Sainct* Mathewe, and vppon his wordes rehearsed by *Sainct* | Luke, our Lorde veray playnly declared vnto his Apostelles | that in that Cuppe was the same bloude of his owne, withe | whiche he woulde ratyfie his newe testament, and whiche | bloude shoulde be sheade vpon the Aultare of the Crosse | for the remyssyon of synnes, not of them selfes alone but | also of manye moo. When our Lorde sayed This is |

no aute antiqm declaracoem ut no de elect. c. pro
inde. c. v. p card. & arch. lic. et circa hoc vide
nota p Jo. an. in prohe. cle. c. v. z. c. v. p greg. &
p paulu n semp hec dicto approbat ea que precess
erit. Ut not. W. de pen. z rem. c. fi. c. v. in cle.
pronunctatur. i. tolleret. prout al de hoc & multi
plici spitu huius dictois pnuncare. no. in . . . omnis
inter lex. p Jo. vel dic pnunctat. i. concedat. sic al
exponitur. de eta. & qua. c. i.o p card. & arch. li. cj.
publice. cora iudice. vel pu. i. notorie vel palam
de sponsis. c. i. v. pu. p arch. li. cj. pu. nam fieri
id dicit. qd omnibz patet. ff. de suspectis tu. l. i.
§. consequens. Sz in hoc casu puto pu. debere intelligi
respcu no solum iudicis si fori seu curie. & multitu
dinis ibi psencium put al no. in. c. fi. de si. z ho
cle. v. pu. p W. in cle. et sic pu. dicit. cora pplo
vel pu. i. commune. cora multis. Ad quod vide nota
in constitucoe otonis. licz v. pu. p Jo. de atona. pius
s. anteqm illud officium exerceat. per tenniu. de
iure civili limitat. quinquennu. ut pz in pohemio. ff.
§. si qr solitu. z le. z no. C. de advo. divsorz iudic
l. iubemus. Nec video qs moveat statuente ad limita
coem maoris temporis nisi intelligas hoc. ut. s. ad
advocet in curijs pedaneis & inferioribz. ubi non
tractatur tam graves s. modici ponderis. In talibus
namqz sufficere vi. qd aliquis sit exercitatus i cau
& sciat practica cu speculativa p trienniu ut hic &
facit ad hoc C. de iudicijs. l. certi iuris. In curijs
tn maoribz & in quibz tractantur ardue cause. opo
est advocatus fulcis maiori scia. ut dicit l. iubemus
cu concordancijs. Audivit. ut discipulus sub magistro
sive doctore. nec refert ut vi. an in studio generali

nomeii & civile. fidem. i. probacoem. testio. s.
p testimoniu doctoris. sub quo studuit. C. de advo.
divsorz iudicioz. l. nemi circa me. . . . . . vidit cora
in hoc casu sufficere lins testimonalis cancellarij
universitatis in qua studuit vel potuit hoc probare
p testes. facti evidencia. qr potuis ad examen
no est repertus habilis n in iure pitus respcu tep
is tenniu. iuramento. sic qd sufficit ad effectum
qd pnunctat. pu. postulare deficiente condigno
testiomo vel facti evidencia. si iuret p tenniu
se audivisse ius canonicu & civile. cum debita
diligecia. Sz quero qs operabitur psticio huius
iuramenti. cu p facti evidencia apparet insuffi
ciens. Dic qd operabitur ad hoc. ut p illud pbet se p
tenniu audivisse iura. no tn ad hoc. qd ppica
iudex teneatur eu admittere ad officium advoca
di. na licz iudex psttio huiod iuramento possit
eu admittere. non tn ad hoc tenetur. qr no eoqz
iudicis potestati committitur iuris necitati sup
ponitur. ff. de iudic. l. no quicqz. Et in eventu
quo debeat in advocatum admitti. debet cora pst
tare iuramentu ab advocatis in sua admissioe
exigi consuetu. de quo le. in constitucoe ottoboni
laudabilem. & C. de iudic. l. rem. no novam
§. primi aute causaz

De procuratoribus
Exhor Johes pecham
iensis et J. Statuimus
ut nullus decanus seu archidi

or Hic est calix novu testamentum in meo sanguine, qui
pro vobis & pro multis fundetur in remissionem peccatoru.
This is the Chalyce the newe testamente in
my bloude, whiche shalbe sheade for you and
for many for the remyssion of synnes. Here
you se that by the wordes of our Saviour rehearsed by
St. Mathewe, and uppon his wordes rehearsed by St.
Luke, our Lorde verey playnly declared unto his Apostelles
that in that Cuppe was the same bloude of his owne, withe
whiche he woulde ratyfie his newe testament, and whiche
bloude shoulde be sheade upon the Aultare of the Crosse
for the remyssyon of synnes, not of them selfes alone but
alsso of manye moo. When our Lorde sayed This is

done his wyll and all her othir systres diden that same: and were of one condicions for as myche as hem dyde thynke that they were of so hyghe and grete blode and parage they wolde not obeye there husbondes, the which wolde have corectyd them wt fayrenes and warned hem to be well demened to there bothe worship and honowres:· But it was all for nouthte for ther was no remedy where for

n the olde ~~grete~~ grete cite of Troye there was a myghty man called Eneas a man of grete power the whiche fledde wt moche people when the cite of Troye was distroyed be hem of Grece & this Eneas came in to Lumbardy where off the kyng was called Latyne that werryd wt an other kyng called Tirocelyne & dyde moche harme and anger and the kyng Latyne heryng of the myghte and worthynes of this Eneas welcomed hym wt moche honoure and worship and helde wt hym and this Eneas helpyd kyng Latyne in his werres and Eneas

And a non aftyr þe Bretons all þey went to London // And crowned þe Constantyne and made hym kyng off þis lande // And þe bushops Gosselyne sette þe crowne on hys hed and ~~ane~~ anoynted hym as þe ffaith for a kyng to done // And þe he began . . . done þt kyng Constantyne when he was crowned // And anone aftyr he spoused his wyffe þat was cousynes off þe Bretons // And he begatt .iii. sones upon her // the ffirste man called Constance // þe seconde Aurylius

PLATES 21–24. The Handwriting of Individual Scribes

21. VARIATIONS IN THE HANDWRITING OF A SINGLE SCRIBE WITHIN THE SAME MS.

London: Society of Antiquaries. MS. 223, fols. 1v, 2v, and 30v.

'The Brut' in English (*v.* note to Pl. 12 (ii)), ending abruptly at chapter 71 (ed. Brie, E.E.T.S. (o.s.), 131, p. 67, line 24). For the text of these three plates compare Brie's edition as follows: (i) not in Brie, (ii) p. 5, lines 5 ff., (iii) p. 46, lines 33 ff.

(A similar development can be traced in the handwriting of letters written by the same correspondent over a number of years: e.g. the hand of Sir John Paston II, cf. Brit. Mus. Additional MS. 34888, fols. 189–90 (dated 1461) with Brit. Mus. Additional MS. 27445, fol. 90 (dated 1475); and the hand of Edmund Paston, cf. Brit. Mus. Additional MS. 34889, fol. 130 (dated 1471) with Brit. Mus. Additional MS. 27446, fol. 93 (datable after 1487).)

(i). fol. 1v.

The scribe has commenced writing a calligraphic well-spaced Secretary book hand of the second half of the fifteenth century. Compare with Pl. 12 (ii) and note here the emphasis on calligraphy. The letters have been carefully formed, and broken strokes have been scrupulously observed in the lobes of **a**, **d** (1, 'and'), and **o** (2, 'one'), the stem of **c** (2, 'condicions'), and the shaft of **t** (3, 'thynke'). The ascender of **d** is simple. The Secretary forms of **g** and **r** are constant. The hand is very formal, and there is little evidence of currency. Note calligraphic emphasis on horns: e.g. on final **s** (1, 'systres').

done his wyll and all her othir systres diden that | same: and were of one condicions for as myche as | hem dyde thynke that they were of so hyghe and | grete bloode and parage they wolde not obeye there | husbondes/ the which wolde haue corectyd them wt | fa⌜y⌝renes and warned' hem to be well demened' to | there bothe worship*es* and honowres:. But it was | all for noughte for ther was no remedy. wherefor |

(ii). fol. 2v.

The hand has already become more current and less formal. Letter forms are linked together, and many of the broken strokes have been resolved by the currency of the writing (cf. **c** in 5, 'called' with that in 2, 'condicions' in (i) above). The hand is less compact, most noticeable perhaps in the treatment of **h.** **e** is frequently replaced by the cursive form (9, 'helde'), and the ascender of **d** is frequently looped (6, 'dyde'). The Secretary form of final short-**s** has been replaced by the more current Anglicana form (1, 'was'), and the Anglicana form of **g** has appeared alongside its Secretary counterpart (7, 'heryng').

(I)n the olde [Cete] cite of ⌜grete⌝ **troye** there was a myghty man | called. **Eneas.** a man of grete power the whiche fledde | wt moche people when the Cite of **troye** was distroyed | be hem of grece. ⁊ this **eneas** came into lumbardy | where off the kyng' was called. **latynie** that werryd | wt an other kyng' called **Turocelyne** ⁊ dyde moche harme | and anger// and the kyng' **latynie** heryng' [.] of the myghte | and wordynes of this. **Eneas** welcomed hyme wt moche | honouure and worship and helde wt hym and this | **Eneas** helpyd kyng' **latynie** in his werres and **eneas** |

(iii). fol. 30v.

The scribe has now abandoned all pretence to calligraphy, and any attempt to observe Secretary models. The hand is now a typical example of late-fifteenth-century Anglicana (cf. Pl. 3 (ii), although here the hand is not compact, but tends to sprawl across the page). The letters exhibit the typical irregularity in the direction of the strokes (4, 'croune'), and variation in size (1, 'batayle'; 7, 'constauntyne').

(A)nd anon aftyr þe batayle all þey went | to **london**// and crowned þ*er* [cos] **constantyne** | and made hym kyng' off þis lande// and þe | bushope **Gosselyne** sette þe croune on hys hed | and [ano] anoyntted hym as be Falleth' | For a kyng' to bene// and þo he began crystyn| dome þis kyng' **constauntyne** when he was | crowned// and anone aftyr he spoused his | wyffe þorow counseyle off þe **brytou*n*s**// and | he begat .iii. sonnes vppon her// the Fyrste | men called **constaunce**// þe secunde **aury** |

22. THE VERSATILITY OF AN AMATEUR SCRIBE: ROGER WALL.

(On Wall's career *v.* Emden, *BRUO*. For accounts of scribes who regularly used more than one script *v.* A. I. Doyle, 'The Work of a Late Fifteenth Century English Scribe, William Ebesham', *Bulletin of the John Rylands Library*, xxxix (1957), p. 298; R. A. B. Mynors, 'A Fifteenth Century Scribe: T. Werken', *Transactions of the Cambridge Bibliographical Society*, i (1950), p. 97; also P. J. Lucas, 'John Capgrave, O.S.A., 1393–1464, Scribe and "Publisher" ', ibid., v (1969), 1–35. Cf. notes to Pls. 6 (ii) (Stephen Doddesham), 7 (i), and Pls. 19–20.)
7 (i), and Pls. 19–20.)

(i). 1454. Shrewsbury School, MS. viii, fol. 82^v^.

William Lyndwood, 'Provinciale seu Constitutiones Anglie' (*v.* note to Pl. 20 (i)). Printed at Oxford, 1679; text of this plate, ibid., pp. 341–3.

Written by Roger Wall in 1454 (see *Transactions of Salop Archaeological and Natural History Soc.*, 2nd series, ix (1897), p. 296).

The text is in a well-written Secretary hand. The proportions, splay, simplified letter forms (e.g. 3, 'alios'), and treatment of the ascenders are characteristic of the mid fifteenth century (cf. Pls. 10 (ii); 12 (i)). The occasional emphasis on horns (e.g. on **e** in 2, 'minime'), and the calligraphic formation of the minims are conservative, and are more characteristic of a slightly earlier date (cf. Pl. 11 (ii)).

The headings are not in the well-written Textura which one might expect from Wall's competence in the script (cf. the next plate), but in a somewhat crude attempt to produce a Bastard, or Fere-textura hand.

vt ipsa decetero inuiolabiliter obseruentur ex hoc inhibere | minime intendentes quin possint pretacti si voluerint | ad alios communes penitenciarios dum tamen id constet pro sacramento | penitencie conuolare/ **Simon Sudbury** | **Confessiones** mulierum extra[1] | velum audiantur | et patulo quantum ad visum non quantum ad auditum. Mo-|neantur eciam laici statim in principio quadragesime confiteri et cito | post lapsum/ ne peccatum pondere suo ad aliud trahat/ | ¶ Item nullus sacerdos nomine penitencie totalis uel particularis | missas presumat iniungere consulere tamen potest **¶ Idem** | **In** confessionibus et predicacionibus sepius laicis inculcetur | et precipue in maioribus solemnitatibus quod omnis[2] | commixtio maris et femine nisi per matrimonium excu|setur est mortale peccatum. ¶ Et si in denunciacione huius | salubris doctrine sacerdos necligens inuentus fuerit tanquam | fornicator uel consenciens fornicacionibus canonice puniatur
Idem |[3] **Confessiones** ter in | Anno audiantur | Ter communicari moneantur in pascha/ in pentecho|ste/ et in natiuitate domini. Prius tamen preparent se per aliquam | abstinenciam de consilio sacerdotis faciendam. Quicumque | autem semel in Anno adminus proprio non fuerit confessus sacerdoti | et adminus ad pascha sacramentum eukaristie non recepit nisi | de consilio sacerdotis duxerit abstinendum/ viu⟨e⟩ns ab | ingressu ecclesie arceatur et mortuus careat cristiana sepul-|

[1] 'A' in margin. [2] 'B' in margin. [3] 'C' in margin.

(ii). Mid fifteenth century. Glasgow: University Library, Hunterian MS. U. 5. 3 (Young and Aitken, no. 263), fol. 41^r^.

Thomas of Elmham, 'Liber metricus de Henrico Quinto' (ed. C. A. Cole, *Memorials of Henry V, King of England*, RS. 11 (London, 1858); text of this plate, ibid., p. 166).

Written by Wall probably in the mid fifteenth century. Note Wall's characteristic inscription written at the foot of the page in the same hand as the text.

A competent Textura Quadrata. Note the characteristic features of this script. Curved strokes have been entirely replaced by heavily traced vertical strokes, broken at head and foot where necessary in order to preserve the dimensions of the letter forms (e.g. the letter **o**, 1, 'theothocos'). The body of the letters is of uniform height. Ascenders and descenders are very short. **f**, long-**s**, and **r** do not descend below the line of writing. Note the degree of precision and discipline in the calligraphy of the hand, revealed in the attempt to achieve uniformity in tracing the strokes. The ornamental nature of the script is further emphasized by the addition of otiose hairlines to final letters.

There were three principal varieties of Textura. The chief distinction between them lies in the method of finishing the feet of the minims and the mainstrokes of **r**, **f**, and long-**s**. In Textura Prescissa the feet of these strokes were 'squared off'; in Textura Quadrata (as here) the feet were finished with short oblique strokes; whereas in Textura Semi-quadrata (Pl. 19 (i)) they were either rounded off or left unfinished.

Ornes theothocos. flore virente nouo.
Nuncia sacra tibi. que contulit angelus angli.
Almiphonis resonent. perpetuanda tonis.
Cara caro Cristi. caro fit tua munere caro.
Huius nos releuet. mors sacra. gente sacra.
Vera fides vireat. per te qua corruat orbis.
Summa supersticio. perfidieque status.

Nomen versifici. qui poscit certificari.
Litterulis capitum. sillabicare potest. Thomas Elmham Monachus

sillabicando petat[1]

Constat Magistro Rogero Walle.
Claudatur muro. constat liber iste Rogero.

[1] Added in the hand of Thomas Martin of Palgrave (1697–1771).

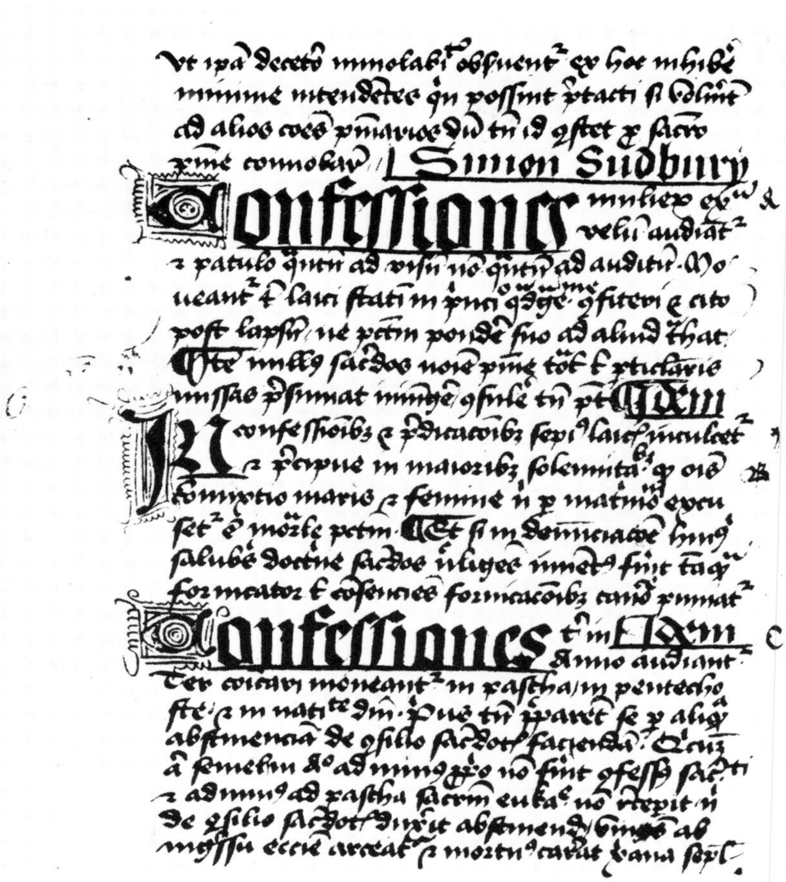

ut ipa decreto inviolabilit' observent' ex hoc inhibe-
mus ne intendentes qui possint presentati si volunt
ad alios curatos parochianos [illegible]
[illegible] | Simon Sudbury

Confessiones mulierum [illegible] audiat
[illegible]

Confessiones [illegible]
[illegible]

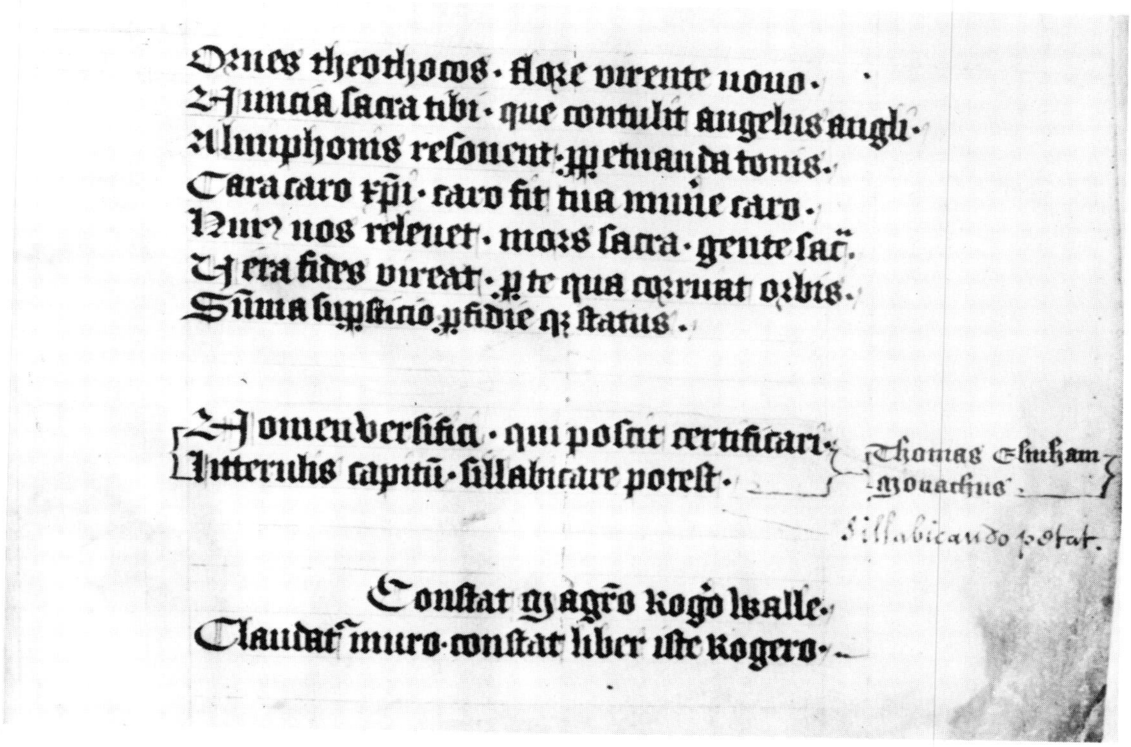

Omnes theothocos · flore virente novo ·
Nuncia sacra tibi · que contulit angelus angli ·
Alimphonis resonent ; pretiuanda tonis ·
Cara caro xpi · caro fit tua munie caro ·
Huius nos releuet · mors sacra · gente sac.
Vera fides vireat · per te qua corruat orbis ·
Summa supplicio perfidie q3 status ·

Nomen versifici · qui posuit certificari ·
Litteruhs capitu · sillabicare potest ·

Thomas Elmham monachus

sillabicando potest

Constat quod agro Rogo Walle ·
Claudatur muro · constat liber iste Rogero ·

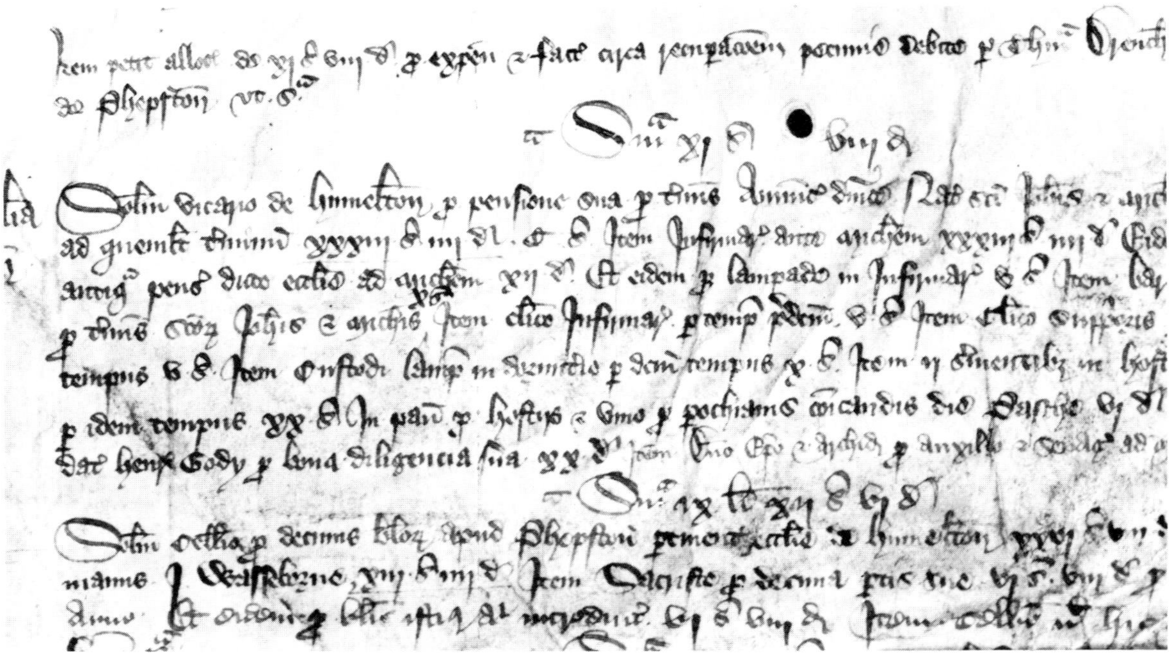

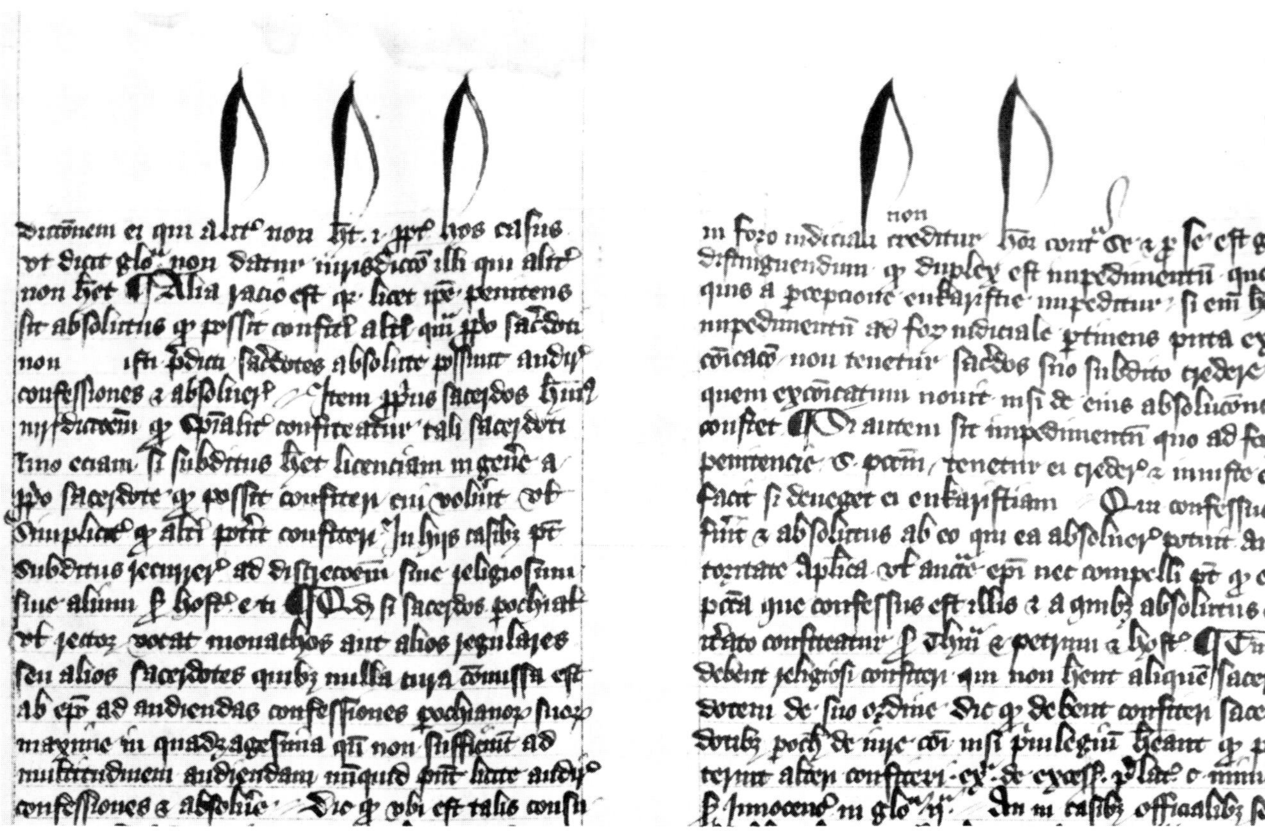

23. THE DOCUMENT HAND AND THE BOOK HAND OF JOHN CLIVE, MONK OF WORCESTER.

(i). 1412–13. Worcester: Cathedral Muniments, Account Roll, C222.

Account Roll of John Clive as *Hostillarius* of Worcester Cathedral Priory, showing the beginning of the *allocationes* (allowances or expenses) section for the year 1412–13.

Typical example of a well-written Anglicana hand of the kind found in documents of this date. Although it contains occasional Secretary forms such as **a** and **s** (e.g. 10, 'bona', 9, 'tempus'), this hand betrays less influence of the new calligraphy than do some of the contemporary book hands (cf. Pl. 2 (ii)). Ascenders and descenders are frequently longer than in the book hands.

(ii). Probably 1412. Oxford: Bodleian Library, MS. Hatton 11 (*SC*. 4132), fol. 90ʳ.

'Regimen Animarum', a manual for parish priests (*v.* W. A. Pantin, *The English Church in the Fourteenth Century* (Cambridge, 1955), pp. 203–5).

Written by John Clive, probably in 1412. The words 'Iohannes de Clyua monachus' appear in the initial on fol. 4ʳ. On fol. 34ʳ there is a series of directions for finding the movable feasts, Easter, the prime or golden number, the Indicts, the Epacts, and coincident feasts for the years 1404 to 1456.

A cross appears in the margin against the entry relating to 1413. It was common practice for a scribe who was copying such a series to indicate in this way the Easter next following (*v.* addenda to *SC.* 16923 and *SC.* 21941 in vol. v, pp. xii and xxii). This would suggest that Clive copied the manuscript some time in the latter part of 1412.

Compare with the previous plate and note how Clive has modified his handwriting for copying the book. Although the model he had in mind was clearly Anglicana Formata, he has in fact incorporated features from all three varieties of Anglicana, a fact which gives to the hand its individual appearance. The most obvious difference between this and the hand used for the accounts is the greater punctiliousness and attention to detail. The mainstrokes of letters are broken at the foot, even in medial positions (e.g. **l** in a, 5, 'absolute', compare previous plate 10, 'diligencia'), as well as the strokes forming the lobes of letters (e.g. **g** in b, 2, 'distinguendum'). In the formation of the minims, sometimes he follows the practice of Bastard Anglicana (a, 1, 'qui', cf. Pl. 7 (ii)), but for the most part he follows the practice of Anglicana Formata (a, 6, 'Item', cf. Pl. 5 (ii)). Note the presence of short **r**, frequent in Anglicana Formata at this period (cf. Pl. 6 (i)), alongside the long-tailed form (b, 1, 'creditur', a, 11, 'recurrere'). The relationship between the height of the ascenders and the size of the body of the letter forms is more characteristic of the less formal variety of Anglicana (*v.* p. xvii). Note also the details of calligraphy, especially in the hairlines added to final letters (e.g. the flourish on final **r**, a, 7, 'confiteatur').

(col. a) diccionem ei qui aliter non habet id est propter hos casus | vt dicit glosa non datur iurisdiccio illi qui aliter | non habet ¶ Alia racio est quia licet ipse penitens | sit absolutus quod possit confiteri alteri quam proprio sacerdoti | non isti predicti sacerdotes absolute possunt audire | confessiones et absoluere //Item proprius sacerdos habemus (*for* habet) | iurisdiccionem quod specialiter confiteatur tali sacerdoti | immo eciam si subditus habet licenciam in genere a | proprio sacerdote quod possit confiteri cui uoluerit vel | simpliciter quod alteri poterit confiteri In hiis casibus potest | subditus recurrere ad discrecionem siue (ad) religiosum | siue alium secundum hostiensem eodem titulo ¶ Quod si sacerdos parochialis | vel rector vocat monachos aut alios regulares | seu alios sacerdotes quibus nulla cura commissa est | ab episcopo ad audiendas confessiones parochianorum suorum | maxime in quadragesima quando non sufficiunt (*for* sufficiat) ad | multitudinem audiendam numquid possunt licite audire | confessiones et absoluere // Dic quod vbi est talis consu-|

(col. b) in foro iudiciali ⌜non⌝ creditur homini contra se et pro se est ergo | distinguendum quod duplex est impedimentum quo | quis a percepcione eukaristie impeditur/ si enim habet | impedimentum ad forum iudiciale pertinens puta ex|communicacio(nem) non tenetur sacerdos suo subdito credere | quem excommunicatum nouit nisi de eius absolucione | constet ¶ Si autem sit impedimentum quo ad forum | penitencie/ scilicet peccatum/ tenetur ei credere et iniuste ei | facit si deneget ei eukaristiam // Qui confessus | fuerit et absolutus ab eo qui ea absoluere potuit. Auc-|toritate Apostolica vel auctoritate episcopi nec compelli potest quod ea | peccata que confessus est illis et a quibus absolutus est | iterato confiteatur secundum Thomam et petrum et Hostiensem ¶ Cui | debent religiosi confiteri qui non habent aliquem sacer-|dotem de suo ordine Dic quod debent confiteri sacer-|dotibus parochialibus de iure communi nisi priuilegium habeant quod po-| terint alteri confiteri. extra. de excessibus prelatorum. capitulo. nimis iniqua[1] | secundum Innocencium in glosa iiª. // An in casibus officialibus seu |

[1] *Decretalium* V. Tit. xxxi. cap. xvi.

24. AN ENGLISH AND A FOREIGN SCRIBE COMPARED.

(i). 1448. Oxford: Magdalen College, MS. Lat. 154, fol. 30^{r}, col. b.

Thomas Dockyng, 'Commentarius in S. Pauli ad Galatas Epistolam' (Stegmüller, *Bibl.* 8101; *v.* A. G. Little, *Franciscan Papers, Lists and Documents* (Manchester, 1943), p. 98; and Emden, *BRUO.*).

Written by Thomas Colyngborne in 1448 (fol. 18^{r}, 'Anno regni regis henrici vi^{ti} xxv, xxi Iunii Thomas Colyngborne senior'). Colyngborne also wrote Magdalen Coll., MS. Lat. 156. Both books were given by John Dygon, and Joanna, a recluse at S. Botolph's Bishopsgate, London, to Thomas Grenewode with reversion to the college. On Dygon, *v.* Emden, *BRUO.* The heading is in Dygon's hand.

Colyngborne was a professional scribe (on fol. 18^{r} there is a note 'this quyer is half writt' vnpay⟨d⟩ aftir the copie'), but compare with the following plate and note here the mixture of Anglicana and Secretary, and the absence of fluency, which indicate the kind of confusion that could be caused by the presence of two models. The characteristic graphs of both scripts appear: **a** (21, 'amicabiliter'), **g** (19, 'cogenter argumentando'), **r** (5, 'persuadere curat'), and **s** (14, 'dicens', 15, 'vultus'). Note also the confusion of the hooked ascenders proper to Anglicana and the small loops of Secretary (21, 'amicabiliter'). The size of the letters varies (19, 'argumentando').

Mixed hands are difficult to date. If this hand were undated, however, the scribe's treatment of ascenders would afford a clue. Alongside the tall hooked ascenders proper to Anglicana, he frequently uses short ascenders with small loops, which are characteristic of Secretary hands of the mid fifteenth century (cf. Pls. 10 (ii); 12 (i)). This detail would reinforce a general impression of the probable date created by the size of the hand, and by the predominant 'threadlike' quality, or evenness in the dimensions of the strokes.

The note in the margin suggests that like his colleague Colyngborne had considerable difficulty in reading his exemplar.

¶ dockyng' super Epistolam | Ad Galathas. 4^{m}. capitulum
sicut eciam stans iacentem erigere non potest nisi a rigore | sui status inclinetur ut iacentem leuet/ quia dum recti-|tudo stantis a iacente discrepat eum nequaquam leuat | sic exhortator (*for* exhortatur) efficaciter vt conuenienter persuadere non potest | nisi similitudinem eorum quibus persuadere curat conformiter | assumere studeat hinc est quod qui dolentem efficaciter | vult consolari:· necesse est vt dolentis animum in se studeat | transformare sicut docet gregorius[1] 3 libro moralium dicens. Ordo conso-|lacionis est vt cum uolumus afflictum quempiam a merore | suspendere:· studeamus prius eius luctui merendo concordare. do-|lentem namque non potest consolari qui non concordat | dolori. quia eo ipso quo a merentis affliccione[2] discrepat | minus ab illo recipitur cui (*for* qui) mentis qualitate separatur. | Idem senciebat poeta[3] dicens/ vt ridentibus arrident | ita fle(n)tibus assint humani vultus. si vis me flere dol-| endum est primum ipsi tibi. tunc tua me infortunia ledunt/ | **Fratres obsecro vos.** Huc usque ab illo loco **Nos** | **natura iudei** ostensum est obseruacionem legalium nichil | prodesse ad salutem. cogenter argumentando. hic ostendit | illud idem suauiter [trib]-blandoendo (*for* blandiendo) et habet hec pars duo quia primo | blanditur amicabiliter alliciendo 2° suauiter admonendo | ibi **Bonum autem imitamini** In parte prima quia in precedentibus vsus est |

[1] In margin 'gregorius'.

[2] In margin a hand with arm points to the following comment made by the scribe: 'no(ta) optime pro amore | ihesu cristi quo modo ego | affligor in scripcione | libri.'

[3] In margin 'Poeta'.

(ii). Probably 1442. Oxford: Balliol College, MS. 30, fol. 119^{v}, col. b.

Thomas Dockyng, 'Commentarius in S. Pauli Epistolas' (Stegmüller, *Bibl.* 8101–10; *v.* Little, op. cit.).

Written probably in England in 1442 for William Gray by a German or Netherlandish scribe (on fol. 308^{v} the ejaculation 'Maria hilff' has been inserted into the text at the foot of the page), *v.* R. A. B. Mynors, *Catalogue of the MSS of Balliol College, Oxford* (Oxford, 1963), pp. xxvi and 21.

Typical example of the book hand developed by the scribes in northern Germany and the Low Countries from the continental form of the script which in England is called Secretary. G. I. Lieftinck, 'Pour une nomenclature de l'écriture livresque de la période dite "gothique"', *Nomenclature des écritures livresques* (Paris, 1954), calls this kind of handwriting *Littera cursiva textualis* ibid., (fig. 21).

The note in the margin indicates that this scribe was labouring under the same difficulties as Colyngborne, but note here the controlled fluency of this hand due to the absence of two models. The hand is upright without any trace of splay. Note the forms of **r** (4–5, 'confidencior) and upright **g** with square lobe, which are characteristic of the handwriting of teutonic scribes (*v.* M. B. Parkes, 'A Fifteenth Century Scribe: Henry Mere', *Bodleian Library Record*, vi (1961), p. 658, and n. 1).

da precepta et causas discuciendas[1] | ¶ Consequenter prosequitur 2^{am} utili-|tatem que scilicet est uerbi dei multi|plicacio siue eius audacior et con-|fidencior predicacio et sunt hic tres | partes primo ponit hanc utilita-|tem ¶ 2° quia diuersi diuersimode Cristum | predicauerunt istum diuersitatis modum | distinguit ibi **quidam quidem** 3° os-|tendit hanc diuersitatem cedere ad euuan-|gelii profectum et suum gaudium ibi **qui-| dam enim dum** Ipsam ergo audaciorem | et confidenciorem uerbi dei predica-|cionem ponit dicens **ut plures de fra-|tribus in domino confidentes et cetera** et tan-|guntur hic tria primo scilicet causa istius | audacioris siue confidencioris pre-|dicacionis et est confidencia in do-|mino que tangitur ibi in domino con-|fidentes Deinde occasio eius ibi **in** | **vinculis meis** 3° ipsa audacior pre-|dicacio ex tali causa occasione pro-|

[1] In margin 'magis scripsi sensum quam | uerba quia non poteram | videre propter maculam | exemplaris.'

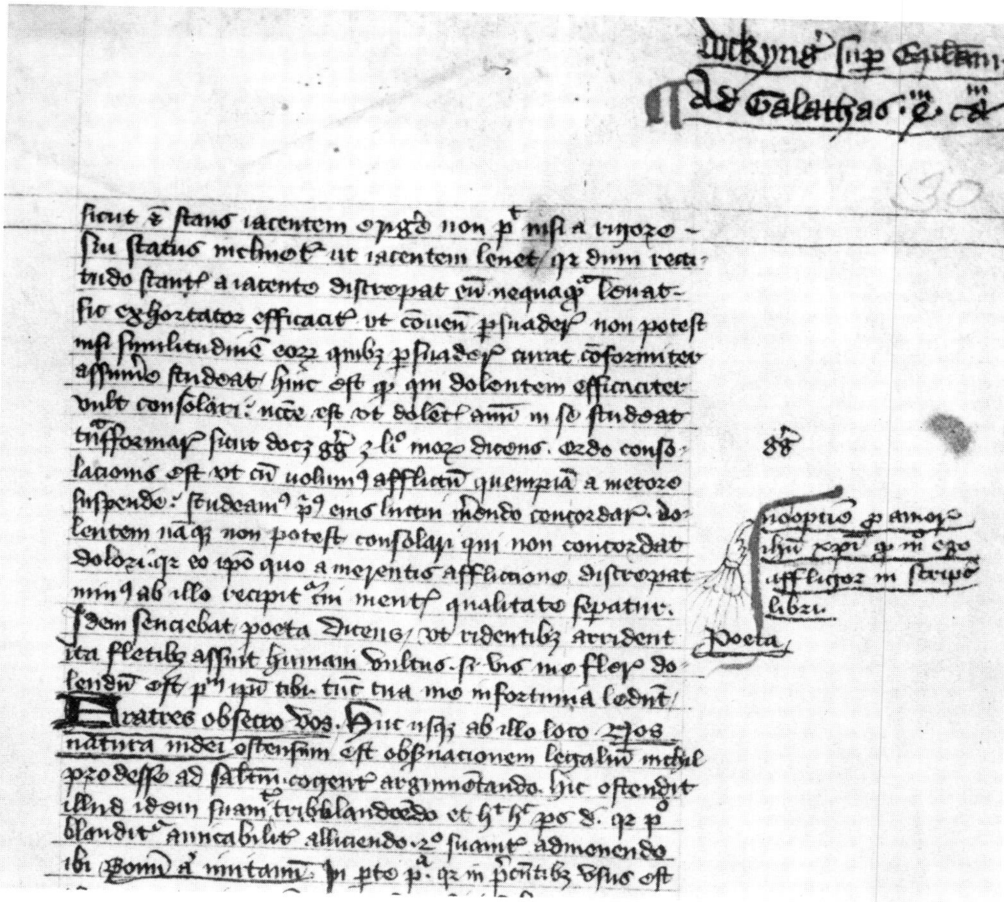

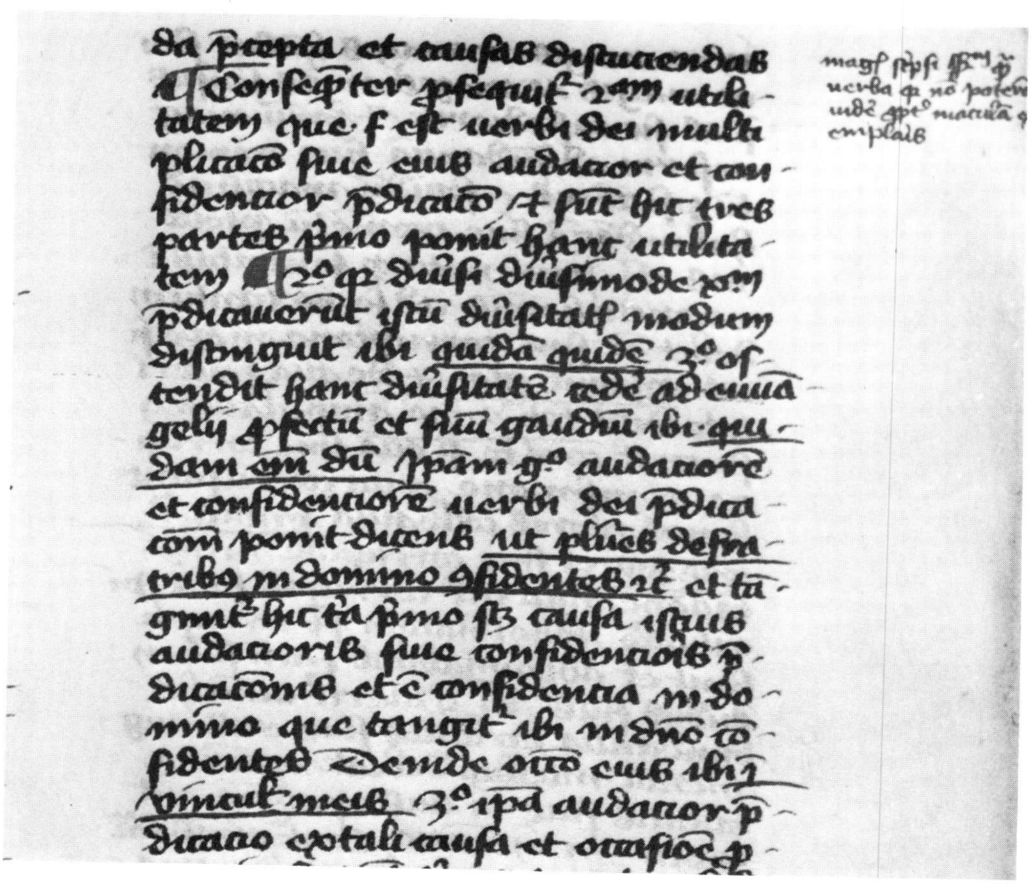

INDEXES

INDEX I: Medieval Persons Connected with the Manuscripts Illustrated

Indicating other manuscripts associated with them, not previously mentioned in the text.

Baron family, arms of, 14 i.
Arms also in Oxford: St John's College, MS. 208; Bodl., MS. Douce 322. William Baron gave MS. Douce 322 to Barking Abbey for the personal use of Petronella Wrattisley.

B., J., copied 2 ii (1419).

Beccles, fr Peter de, Carmelite friar, 'fecit scribi' 5 i (1380).

Bobych, J., copied 3 i.

Bozoun, Simon, Prior of Norwich Cathedral Priory, owned 4 ii.
Also owned Cambridge: Corpus Christi College MSS. 264, 407; Bodl. MS. Fairfax 20; *v. Giraldi Cambrensis Opera*, RS, v, p. xxxix, n.

Clive, John, monk of Worcester, copied 23 i, ii (1412–13).

Colyngborne, Thomas, copied 24 i (1448).
Also copied Oxford: Magdalen Coll. MSS. lat. 145, 156; Brit. Mus. MS. Harley 612; and cf. Oxford: Merton Coll. MS. 153, fols. 139–end.

Crome, Walter, owned and copied part of 11 ii (1446).
Also owned Cambridge: University Library, MSS. Ee. 1. 25; Ii. 1. 28–9; Ii. 3. 9; Ii. 4. 13; Ii. 4. 23; Ii. 4. 29; Cambridge: Kings College, MS. 9; Corpus Christi College, MS. 68 (which he gave to Cambridge University); Gonville & Caius College, MSS. 114, 129, 131, 342, 395 (which he gave to Gonville Hall).

Croucher (Crowcher), John (*v.* Emden, *BRUC.*), owned 1 i.
Gave Cambridge: University Library, MS. Ii. 3. 21 to the University.

Darker, William, monk of Sheen, copied 8 ii.

Doddesham, Stephen, monk of Sheen, copied 6 ii (1475). Cf. p. 22.
Also copied Cambridge: Trinity College, MS. B. 15. 16; Brit. Mus. Additional MS. 10053; Bodl. MSS. Bodley 423 B, 549 B, Rawlinson A 387 B.

Dygon, John, recluse of Sheen, owned and annotated 24 i.
Also owned Oxford: Magdalen College, MSS. lat. 60, 77, 79, 93, 156, 177; St. John's College, MS. 77.

Eyton, Hugo, Subprior of S. Albans, owned 19 ii.
On Eyton *v.* R. W. Hunt, 'The library of the Abbey of St Albans', *Medieval Scribes, Manuscripts & Libraries: Essays Presented to N. R. Ker*, ed. M. B. Parkes and Andrew G. Watson (London 1978), pp. 254–5, and for books borrowed by him, pp. 274–5.

Fortescue, Sir John, arms of, 8 i.

Gloucester, Thomas, Duke of (d. 1397), owned 5 ii; *v.* also p. xvi, n. 2.

Gray, William, bishop of Ely (1454–78) owned 24 ii.
On Gray and his books *v.* R. A. B. Mynors, *Catalogue of the MSS. of Balliol College, Oxford* (Oxford, 1963).

Grenewode, Thomas, owned 24 i.
Other MSS. given by Dygon (q.v.) to Grenewode with reversion to Magdalen College, Oxford are Oxford: Magd. Coll., MSS. lat. 156, 177.

Holbrook, (Holbroke), John, owned 5 i.
Wrote Brit. Mus. Egerton MS. 889; also owned London: Royal College of Physicians, MS. 390 (which he also gave to Peterhouse).

Holme, Thomas, copied 18 i (1467).

Joanna, recluse at St Botolph's, Bishopsgate, see 24 i.
Her name is also associated with that of John Dygon (q.v.) in Oxford: Magdalen College, MS. lat. 77.

Kyngorn, Robert de, copied 13 i (1470).
Scottish notary: *v. Register of the Great Seal*, ii, no. 3504 (dated 1465) (ex informacione Dr. R. Lyell).

Maydeston, fr Simon, monk of St Augustine's, Canterbury, owned 11 i.
His name also appears in Brit. Mus. Royal MS. 10 B xiv.

Maynesford, John, copied 17 ii.

Meydistane, fr Thomas, canon of Leeds Priory (Kent), owned 4 i.

Multon, Edmund de, copied 19 i (1355).

Norfolk. John, copied 6 i (*c.* 1445).
List of books given by him to All Souls College pr. N. R. Ker, *Records of All Souls College Library, 1437–1600*, Oxford Bibliographical Society, N.S. xvi (1971), 215.

Percy family, arms of, 15 ii.

Russell, John, bishop of Lincoln (1480–94), copied 18 ii (1491/2).
Also owned Oxford: New College, MSS. 138, 211, 263, 267, 271, 274 (which he gave to the college, together with printed books); Lincoln College, MS. 25 (which he gave to that college). Owned Brit. Mus. Royal MSS. 14 C vii, 15 A xxi; Oxford: New College, MSS. 195, 196. His pontifical is now Cambridge: University Library, MS. Mm. 3. 21.

Sinclair family, arms of, 13 ii.
On some of their books *v.* N. R. Ker, *Medieval Manuscripts in British Libraries*, ii, 1–2, and nn.

Snetisham, John, owned 3 i.
Also owned Bodl. MSS. Bodley 744, 748.

Stevens, William, copied 12 i.

Wall, Roger, canon of Lichfield, copied 22 i (1454), 22 ii.
Also owned, and, for the most part, copied Cambridge: Trinity College, MS. O. 5. 12; Brit. Mus. Cotton MS. Vitellius A x; London, College of Arms, Arundel MS. 15; Bodl. MSS. Digby 138, e Musaeo 64. Owned Bodl. Auct F. 2. 13. Annotated Cambridge, Corpus Christi College, MS. 369.

Wivil, Robert, bishop of Salisbury (1330–75), owned 7 i.

Wydevile, Richard, 3rd Earl Rivers, owned 15 i.

Wylliot (Wylyot), John, copied 16 ii.

INDEX II: Scribes Mentioned but not Illustrated